SAD PAPAW'S

HERITAGE

KENNY HARMON

Dedication

T his book is dedicated to Babe & Nell Harmon. Their love, religious teachings, character, and strong work ethics have had a great influence in my life! Special thanks to Donna Harmon Elmore, Peggy Harmon Brawley, Anita Harmon Powell, Rhonda Pierce O'Malley, Nedra Swinney Smith, Paula Swinney Moore, and Raymond Swinney.

A historical look into the lives of the Harman/Harmon family history, from Kentucky to Missouri to Kansas to Oklahoma.

Table of Contents

Preface

A cool, crisp air was waffling through the town of Dibble, Oklahoma on March 16, 2016. Kenny Harmon was preparing his tasty dish of home fries as the hamburgers sizzled on the grill. He invited his six grandchildren over for a barbecue, an impromptu family get-together. Kelsey was the first to arrive, and as the two chatted over the day's events, it became apparent that the rest of the and children were not coming.

Once the home fries finished, Kelsey and Kenny sat down to eat dinner. Kelsey grabbed her cell phone and snapped a picture of her Papaw taking a bite of his burger. She planned to post it on her Twitter page, with the caption: "dinner with papaw tonight...he made 12 burgers for all 6 grandkids and I'm the only one who showed. love him." This was merely to poke at her brother and her cousins for not showing up for the barbecue. Though minutes later, her brother, Kaleb, arrived and joined them. Not thinking of the harmless picture that she had just taken, the 3 of them carried on with their meal. Fifteen minutes later, she remembered the photo on her phone. In spite of the fact that Kaleb had arrived, she posted it with the original caption.

The image of 'Sad Papaw' was launched into cyberspace. As they finished their burgers and gobbled down their home fries, the photo was being shared by dozens—then hundreds—and then thousands of internet users. The image soared across the country and by morning 'Sad Papaw' would gain thousands of followers and loads of new grandchildren.

Kaleb felt crushed when he learned of the post because, after all, he was there. Would it be too late to recant her statement? According to internet users, he could shout from the moon, "I was there," and it did not matter. They believed that he betrayed Papaw and he could not change their minds.

Not even with the truth.

The Harmon family would become an internet sensation. The attention came as a surprise to this humble family that first settled in the small country town of Dibble, Oklahoma in 1912. The rich history of the Harmon clan (originally spelled Harman') dates back to sweltering days of hard-working farmers traveling west to escape the damage of cyclones and floods and surviving the elements of the Dust Bowl. Any arbitrary turning along the way and the world might never have come to know, Oklahoma's—and now America's—Sad Papaw.

Introduction

As a boy, Kenny adored listening to his grandparents tell him stories of their lives—stories that stretched back to the days of the wild west and onto their travels through Whitley County, Kentucky, Missouri, and Rock, Kansas, all of which eventually led them to Oklahoma. Generations of Harmon family stories carried on through the years in a series of short, heart-warming tales. Their words were streaming like a long thread that he used to weave together his family's history.

He was particularly fond of the history that started with his great-great-great grandparents, Jacob Harman and Mary Shelly Harman—their harsh daily farm lives that began on the green fields of Kentucky, followed by floods, cyclones, war stories, and Indian encounters.

Sad Papaw's Heritage regales in the memories of life on the prairies, sprinkled with American history, the tragedies, and triumphs that his family lived through. Life dragged the hard-working Harmon farmers down the rockiest of roads. As a close-knit family, they survived. They always stood strong by each other's side for family was of the utmost importance.

Chapter 1

The Origins of Hermann/Harman/Harmon

The surname Harman is the Frankish (French) analog of the ancient German name Hermann (Herman), composed of the root words "hari," meaning "army" and "man," meaning "man." The English analog of the name today is Harmon. It is a name of ancient lineage and was mentioned by the Roman Historian Tacitus c. 56-117 A.D., who, in his "Histories" written nearly 2,000 years ago, told of the victory of Arminius (Hermann), Chief of the German tribe Cherusci, over the Roman legions of Publius Quinctilius Varus in the Teutoburgiensis Saltus—the Teutoburg Forest. The Battle of the Teutoberger Wald in 9 A.D. was one of the pivotal battles of world history and Arminius' victory was credited with halting the expansion of the Roman Empire under Augustus Caesar at the Rhine frontier.

It forever prevented the complete subjugation of the Germans by the Romans. And, although Roman legions later won stunning victories over one or another German, Gaulic, or Celtic army, the Romans never succeeded in subduing the German culture or retaining hegemony over the German tribes. Augustus Caesar's plan to move the German frontier to the Elbe was never realized. The battle was a master stroke of military strategy.

Arminius, a military commander, was the leader of the German tribe of the Cherusci who were allied to the Romans. But Varus' harsh, despotic, and arbitrary rule led Arminius to plan a rebellion against Roman rule. He persuaded Varus to lead his three legions and auxiliary troops into the Teutoburg Forest in the late summer of 9 A.D. Arminius was at the head of the rear guard with his Cherusci troops. There, in the forest near modern Detmold, Roman supply wagons mired down and Roman troops broke formation as Arminius had foreseen.

At a signal, German guerrillas stationed in advance by Arminius attacked, the German recruits deserted, and Arminius and his rear guard fell upon the unsuspecting Romans. The Romans, their formations in disarray, were surrounded and cut down by the Germans. Varus vainly tried to march West to safety, but by the second day, the Germans had annihilated all the Roman cavalry. By the third day, some 20,000 Roman infantry had perished and Varus, humiliated, committed suicide.

It is said that Augustus agonized over the defeat by Arminius for the remainder of his life and was heard often to cry in anguish from his quarters at night: "Varus! Give me back my legions!" Hans Bahlow's "Dictionary of German Names," published in English translation by the Max Kade Institute for German American Studies at the University of Wisconsin, Madison, indicates that Herrmann is the preferred spelling today in Bavaria, while Hoermann is the Austrian spelling and Hiermann the Low German spelling.

Harman is a famous and ancient German personal name. Notable German Harman's (Hermann's) have included Hermann Billung, Duke of the Saxons about 950, and Landgrave Hermann of Thuringia, patron of Middle High German poets around 1200. It is mentioned in Goethe's long poem "Hermann and Dorothea" and was revived in popularity as a family name by Klopstock and the Romantics around 1800.

Chapter 2

Part 1
The Long Journey

Johann Michael Hermann was born in the district of Ludwigsburg, Germany in 1669. Johann married Kundigunda Christina Regis. Christina gave birth to Heinrich Adam Hermann in 1700 in Mannheim, Wurttenberg, Germany. Heinrich Adam married Louisa Katrina Mathias.

In 1726 Adam and Louisa and 2-year-old Henry Adam Jr. departed Germany for America. Shortly after boarding the ship "Charlotte", the vessel docked at the Isle of Mann, located between Great Britain and Ireland. While on the Isle Louisa gave birth to Heinrich Henry. The voyage from Great Britain to America normally was 6 to 7 weeks in the mid-1720's.

Henrich Adam and Louisa would have 11 more children after reaching America. Henrich Adam also had 7 siblings that eventually made America their new home. One of those siblings was Jacob Hermann Jr. who was my 5th great grandfather born in 1705 in Mittelgraken, Wurttemburg, Germany.

The Hermann's changed the spelling to Harman or Harmon after becoming Americans. The Hermann's/Harman's/Harmons would become great frontiers men that explored as far west as the Mississippi River. Heinrich Adam Harman founded the first permanent English-speaking settlement west of the Allegheny Mountains in 1745!

Part 2

The Long Journey
By Emory L. Hamilton

From the unpublished manuscript, Indian Atrocities Along the Clinch, Powell and Holston Rivers.

Walter Crockett, County Lieutenant of Militia for Montgomery C 0.,VA , wrote to Governor Edmund Randolph, on February 16, 1789, (1), saying: I take this opportunity to write to you by Captain Sayers, who is going to Richmond on business of his own, to inform you of the state of our frontiers in this county. There has been several of our hunters from the frontier down the Sandy River forty or fifty miles below the settlement on Bluestone on the Clinch, and discovered fresh signs of several parties of Indians, one of the hunters is a brother (2) to Henry Harman, that had the skirmish with them late in the fall, (November 12, 1788) when he and his two sons behaved like heroes, they came immediately in, and warned the frontier settlements, and has applied to me to send out spy's. They say that if there was four Scouts that they could confide in, they would endeavor to plant corn this spring, and stay the summer. Otherwise, Bluestone settlement will break up, and of course the settlement on the head of Clinch will not stand long. I expect as soon as the winter breaks up, that the Indians will commit hostilities on some part of the frontiers of this county the ensuing spring, but God only knows the event. Whatever orders your Excellency and shall be punctually obeyed.

This family of Harman's was of German origin, Adam Heinrich Hermann immigrating to America in 1726, with a brief stop over the Isle of Man, where Henry Harman of this sketch was born. (3) Seven Harman brothers emigrated from Germany together, Jacob, Valentine, Mathias, George, Daniel, John, and Heinrich Adam. They first stopped off in Pennsylvania, and then immigrated to the Shenandoah Valley and some on into North Carolina. At least three of these brothers settled in Southwest

4

Virginia, namely, Heinrich Adam, Valentin and Jacob. They were living in the New River German settlement; the first settlement ever made west of the Alleghenies on the "Western Waters" and was living there prior to 1745. In 1749 Moravian Missionaries conducted the first recorded religious services in Southwest Virginia in the home of Jacob Harman, and Dr. Thomas Walker mentions stopping at the home of Harman on his memorable exploration trip in 1750. Of these three brothers, Valentine and Jacob were both killed by Indians on New River. valentine was killed on Sinking Creek in what is now Giles Co., VA. In a land suit filed in the HighCourt of Chancery in Augusta Co., on the 23rd of July 1807, Taylor vs Harman, (4) Mathias Harman, nephew of the slain Valentine, says: Valentine was killed by the Indians on New River and at the same time his (Mathias') brother, Daniel Harman and Andrew Moser were taken prisoner. Daniel made his escape, but Andrew was held prisoner.

On the 30th of June 1808, Daniel Harman, deposes, in the same land suit, saying: In 1757, Valentine was killed in my presence less than a foot away from me, and I was taken prisoner. Valentine Harman, who was slain, left a widow Mary Harman, but no children.

Jacob Harman lived on Neck Creek in what is now Pulaski Co., VA, on what is known as Spring Dale Farm. In 1757, he, his wife, and one of his sons were murdered by the Indians.

The Harman's of this sketch are the descendants of Heinrich Adam Hermann who emigrated from Germany, who married Louisa Katrina, October 8, 1723. Louisa Katrina died March 18, 1749. The children of this marriage were: [1] Adam Harman, the eldest, born in Germany in 1724; [2] Henry Harman born on the Isle of Man in 1726; [3] George Harman, 1727-1749; [4] Daniel Harman, born Pennsylvania, 1729; [5] Mathias Harman, born near Strausburg, VA, in 1736; [6] Christina Harman, who married Jeremiah Pate, and lived on Little River in Montgomery Co., VA; [7] Catherine Harman who married Ulrich Richards in Rowan Co., NC; [8] Phillipina Harman, who died in 1751; [9] Valentine Harman who settled on the upper Clinch River in 1771, and moved to Lincoln Co., KY, about 1775, and was a member of the Henderson Legislature at Boonesboro in May, 1775; [10] A daughter, name unknown, married a Mr. Looney; [11] Jacob Harman, perhaps the Jacob who settled in Tazewell Co., VA in 1771. The sons of old Heinrich Adam Hermann, the German emigrant, became great hunters and Indian fighters. While most of them were great hunters, one in particular became one of the noted Long Hunters. It is hard to determine just which son this was, but evidence points to the youngest who was Jacob.

Henry, the second son of Heinrich Adam, owned land in North Carolina, Giles, and Tazewell counties in Virginia. Sometime in the 1750s, he was married to Anna Wilborn of the Moravian settlement in North Carolina and died at his home at "Holly Brook" on Kimberlin Creek in present day Bland Co., VA, in 1822. In 1789, he and his son, Mathias, founded Harman's Station in Kentucky. There is much evidence in the records to prove the great prowess of the Harman's as hunters and Indian fighters. In another land suit in the High Court of Chancery of Augusta Co., Wynn vs English heirs, (5) it is stated: that Henry Harman was in the habit of collecting the men and fighting the Indians. In a land dispute case filed in Augusta (6), Samuel Walker states on May 30, 1805, that he came to the head of Clinch in 1771 and met Valentine Harman. In the same suit Mathias and Daniel Harman, brothers of Henry, state that they were on the land in dispute on a hunting trip in 1760. This statement proves that the Harman's were familiar with the country at the head of Clinch and Bluestone Rivers long before they made actual settlement in the area. In the Minutes of the Court of Montgomery County for May 26, 1790, is found this entry.

Inhabitants of Bluestone ordered to show because why they should not work on that part of the road between Rocky Gap and the head of Clinch. The following were appointed overseers of the road, among who was Captain Henry Harman. Details of the fight between Henry Harman and the Indians are taken from Bickley's History of Tazewell County, with the correct date added.

On the 12th of November 1788, Henry Harman, and his two sons, George and Mathias, and George Draper left the settlement, to engage in a Bear hunt on Tug River. They were provided with pack horses, independent of those used for riding, and on which were to be brought in the game. The country, in which their hunt was to take place, was penetrated by the "warpath" leading to and from the Ohio river; but as it was late in the season they did not expect to meet with Indians.

Arriving at the hunting grounds in the early part of the evening, they stopped and built their camp; a work executed generally by the old man, who might be said to be particular in having it constructed to his own taste. George and Mathias loaded, and put their guns in order, and started to the woods, to look for sign, and perchance kill a buck for the evening repast, while Draper busied himself in hobbling and caring for the horses.

In a short time, George returned with the startling intelligence of Indians! He had found a camp but a short distance from their own, in which partly consumed sticks were still burning. They could not, of course, be at any considerable distance, and might now be concealed near them, watching their every movement. George, while at the camp found leggings, which the old man believed the leggings to have been taken from the body of Capt. Moore after the Moore Massacre. Now old Mr. Harman was a type of frontiersman, in some things, and particularly that remarkable self-possession, which is so often to be met with in new countries, where dangers are ever in the path of the settler. So, taking a seat on the ground, he began to interrogate his son on the dimensions, appearance, etc., of the camp. When he had fully satisfied himself, he remarked, that, "there must be from five to seven Indians", and that they must pack up and hurry back to the settlements, to prevent, if possible, the Indians from doing mischief; and, said he, "if we fall in with them, we must fight them."

Mathias was immediately called in, and the horses repacked. Mr. Harman and Draper, now began to load their guns, when the old man observing Draper, laboring under what is known to hunters as the "buck ague", being that state of excitement, which causes excessive trembling, remarked to him," my son I fear you cannot fight".

The plan was now agreed upon, which was, that Mr. Harman and Draper should lead the way, the pack horses follow them, and Mathias and George bring up the rear. After they had started, Draper remarked to Mr. Harman that he would go ahead, as he could see better than Mr. Harman, and that he would keep a sharp lookout. It is highly probable that he was cogitating a plan of escape, as he had not gone far before he declared he saw the Indians, which proved not to be true. Proceeding a short distance further, he suddenly wheeled his horse about, at the same time crying out, "Yonder they are—behind that log." As a liar is not to be believed when he speaks the truth, so Mr. Draper was not believed this time. Mr. Harman rode on,

7

while a large dog, he had with him, ran up to the log and reared himself upon it, showing no sign of the presence of Indians. At this second, a sheet of fire and smoke from the Indians' rifles completely concealed the log from view, for Draper had really spoken the truth.

Before the smoke had cleared away, Mr. Harman and his sons were dismounted, while Draper had fled with all the speed of a swift horse. There were seven of the Indians, only four of whom had guns; the rest being armed with bows and arrows, tomahawks and scalping knives. As soon as they fired, they rushed on Mr. Harman, who fell back to where his two sons stood ready to meet the Indians.

They immediately surrounded the three white men, who had formed a triangle, each man looking out, or what would have been, with men enough a hollow square. The old gentlemen bid Mathias to reserve his fire, while himself and George fired, wounding, as it would seem, two of the Indians. George was a lame man, from having had white swelling in his childhood, and after firing a few rounds, the Indians noticed his limping, and one who had fired at him, rushed upon him thinking him wounded. George saw the fatal tomahawk raised, and drawing back his gun, prepared to meet it. When the Indian had got within striking distance, George let down upon his head with the gun, which brought him to the ground; he soon recovered, and made at him again, half-bent and head foremost, George sprang up and jumped across him, which brought the Indian to his knees. Feeling for his own knife, and not getting hold of it, he seized the Indians' and plunged it deep into his side. Mathias struck him on the head with a tomahawk and finished the work with him.

Two Indians had attacked the old man with bows, and were maneuvering around him, to get clear fire at his left breast. The Harman's, to a man, wore their bullet pouches on the left side, and with this and his arm he so completely shielded his breast, that the Indians did not fire till they saw the old gentleman's gun nearly loaded again, when one fired on him, and struck his elbow near the joint, cutting one of the principal arteries. In a second more, the fearful string was heard to vibrate, and an arrow entered Mr. Harman's breast and lodged against a rib. He had by this time loaded his gun and was raising it to his face to shoot one of the Indians, when the stream of blood from the wounded artery flew into the pan, and so

8

soiled his gun that it was impossible to make it fire. Raising his gun, however, had the effect to drive back the Indians, who retreated to where the others stood with their guns empty.

Mathias, who had remained an almost inactive spectator, now asked permission to fire, which the old man granted. The Indian at whom he fired appeared to be the chief and was standing under a large beech tree. At the report of the rifle, the Indian fell, throwing his tomahawk high among the limbs of the tree under which he stood.

Seeing two of their number lying dead upon the ground, and two more badly wounded, they immediately made off; passing by Draper, who had left his horse, and concealed himself behind a log.

As soon as the Indians retreated, the old man fell back on the ground exhausted and fainting from the loss of blood. The wounded arm being tied up and his face washed in cold water, soon restored him. The first words he uttered were, "We've whipped them, give me my pipe." This had furnished him, and he took a whiff, while the boys scalped one of the Indians.

When Draper saw the Indians pass him, he stealthily crept from his hiding place, and pushed on for the settlement, where he reported the whole party murdered. The people assembled and started soon the following morning to bury them; but they had not gone far before they met Mr. Harman, and his sons, in too good condition to need burying.

Upon the tree, under which the chief was killed, is roughly carved an Indian, a bow and a gun, commemorative of the fight. The arrows which were shot into Mr. Harman are in possession of some of his descendants. David E. Johnston in his History of the Middle New River Settlements gives a ballad which he says was composed by Captain Henry Harman, herein inserted to show the correct date and add interest to the details of this story.

Capt. Henry Harman's Battle Song

Come all ye bold heroes whose hearts flow with courage,
With respect pay attention to a bloody fray.
Fought by Captain Harman and valiant sons,
With the murdering Shawnees they met on the way.
The battle was fought on the twelfth of November,
Seventeen hundred and eighty-eight.
Where God of his mercy stood by those brave heroes,
Or they must have yielded to a dismal fate.

Oh! Nothing would do this bold Henry Harman,
But down to the Tug River without more delay,
With valiant sons and their noble rifles,
Intending a number of bears to slay.
They camped on Tug River with pleasing contentment,
Till the sign of blood thirsty Shawnees appears,
Then with brave resolution they quickly embark,
To cross the high mountains and warn the frontiers.

Brave Harman rode foremost with undaunted courage,
Nor left his old trail these heathens to shun;
His firm resolution was to save Bluestone,
Though he knew by their sign they were near three to one.
The first salutation the Shawnees did give them,
They saw the smoke rise from behind some old logs;

Brave Harman to fight them then quickly dismounted,
Saying, "Do you lie there, you save, murdering dogs?"

He says, "My dear sons stand by me with courage,
And like heroes fight on till you die on the ground."
Without hesitation they swiftly rushed forward,
They have the honor of taking their hair.
At first by the host of red skins surrounded,
His well pointed gun made them jump behind trees,
At last all slain, but two, and they wounded,
Cherokee in the shoulder, and Wolf in the knees.

Great thanks to the Almighty for the strength and the courage,
By which the brave Harman's triumphed er the foe;
Not the women and children then intended to slaughter,
But the bloody invaders themselves are laid low.
May their generation on the frontiers he stationed,
To confound and defeat all their murdering schemes,
And put a frustration to every invasion,
And drive the Shawnees from Montgomery's fair streams.

Part 3
The Long Journey

The monument in Thorpe, West Virginia where Henry Harman and his sons George and Matthias fought 7 Black Wolf Indians of the Shawnee Tribe on November 12,1788

Heinrich Adam Harman and his wife Louisa Katrina immigrated to America from Germany with their first-born son, Adam, in 1726, along with numerous other Moravian settlers who wanted to escape religious persecution. Along the way, on the Isle of Man, their second son, Henry, was born. The family made their way to the New River area of Virginia and according to a report by surveyors Patton and Buchanan they were the first permanent white settlers in the territory. In 1752 at the age of twenty-six, Henry was appointed constable of the New River Area, a captain of "Troops of Horse" and an overseer of the road. He and his family led the way into the wilderness and their attitudes towards their way of life are exemplified by the final words spoken by his + mother, Louisa Katrina, as she died on March 18, 1749: "My earthly travels are over. I fought a good fight. All men must die, and 1 must leave. Good night all my loved ones". Henry Harman owned land in Tazewell and other counties in southwest Virginia as early as 1754. In 1756, he was commissioned Captain of the King's Militia, a title which stuck with him for the rest of his life Capt. Harman was also dubbed "Old Sky gusty" (Great Warrior) by the Indians. In 1758 he married Anna (Nancy) Williams and they raised nine children in the wilderness. Henry Harman was described by a contemporary as "very tall, of massive frame and very strongly built". In 1787 Captain Henry Harman, being the senior officer, took command of an expedition to rescue some captives that the Shawnee had taken in a raid at Burke's Garden. The Indians were overtaken and Henry planned to attack their camp before dawn. While preparing to charge the Indian camp, he discovered one of his staff, Captain Maxwell wearing a white hunting shirt and told him to take it off because it would be too good a target for the Indians in the dark and the surprise attack would be jeopardized. The order was not obeyed by Maxwell, perhaps because he had no other garment to put on. Maxwell was indeed killed during the first fire; some of the prisoners were killed and scalped, but two Negroes and Mrs. Ingles survived. The area where this encounter took place has since been known as Maxwell's Gap.

The Shawnee frequently raided into western Virginia, crossing the Ohio River, coming up the Kanawha, New River and Little River valleys and across the Blue Ridge Mountains. Their purpose was not only to kill the men and plunder their homes, but to capture women and children to adopt into their families or to exchange prisoners for ransom back to their families or during the Revolutionary War, to the British. "In 1760 a large band of Shawnee invaded the area. Most settlers retreated to their blockhouses and forts, but some lingered at the risk of life and property. The Indians succeeded in capturing a Dutch (German) woman, some horses, pots and other items, and escaped in the direction of Little River. Captain Henry

Harman and his militia were soon on their trail. When the Indians reached a point on Little River in present day Montgomery County, Virginia, where the ground was thickly covered with sedge grass, they stopped to rest and cook a meal. Knowing that most of his militia was raw and undisciplined, Harman placed Thomas Looney and David Lusk, both tried and true soldiers, in charge of the rear to rally and bring them into action as the occasion required. Henry, acting as a vedette, crept forward alone, hoping to surprise the Indians and rescue the prisoners alive. He discovered them behind a large log, eating their meal and laughing and talking with great glee. Pausing not a moment to see where his own men were, or to give a thought to the great danger incurred, he took aim at a tall Indian's back as he stooped to sop his bread and then rose. Harman fired and saw the Indian's back double backward, as a man bends his arm. In an instant the savages sprang behind trees and returned fire. When he left Looney and Lusk, they had told him if the militia faltered, at the first fire of his gun, "They would be at his back". Feeling a hand on his back, he whirled, and Looney and Lusk smiled in his face. The shots from the Indian's rifles cut splinters from the tree they were using for cover, sending splinters into their hair and flesh, which weren't picked out until after their return to the fort. At this critical moment, the militia, several hundred yards away, fired their guns and loudly cheered and hurrahed, which so frightened the Indians that they all fled into the sedge grass. Captain Harman leaped over the log and asked the woman in English, how many Indians there were and received no answer; he asked her in German, and she answered thirty. He told her to throw herself flat on the ground or the Indians would throw back their tomahawks and kill her. Seeing Thomas Looney watching an Indian approaching a path through the grass, he said "Now Thomas, shoot just like you were shooting an old buck". At the fire of Looney's gun, down went the Indian. The militia came stalking in cautiously and were fired upon from the grass. Two of them fell to the ground: one of whom was killed; the other, known as Little Jack (surname forgotten) had the presence of mind to fall to the ground when the other man was hit and thus, he escaped unhurt. The battle continued furiously on both sides, until the Indians, finding seven or eight of their numbers slain, finally gave way on all sides and escaped through the grass, leaving the victorious whites in possession of the field, the rescued prisoner and all the stolen property. Captain Harman returned to the first Indian he had shot and found him sitting with his gun across his lap. Suddenly, moving the muzzle toward his breast, the Indian exclaimed "Wash! Ta!" and fired. He had failed to load enough powder and the ball hung up in the fouled barrel. Harman leaped upon him and dispatched him with his tomahawk. On another occasion, being on horseback and a number of miles from the fort, Henry Harman was waylaid by some Indians and his large bay mare was shot down under him. The mare fell on one of his legs and held him fast to the ground. Seeing the savages rushing upon him with uplifted tomahawks, and being a man of gigantic strength, he drew up the other foot, placed his heel against the mares back and by herculean efforts pushed the huge beast off his leg. Harman leaped to his feet, rifle in hand, and pointing it at their breasts, made them take to the trees for cover. Not giving them time to reload their empty guns, he ran for his life. When they started in pursuit, he again drew his loaded rifle and made them take to the trees, and again ran for his life.

The plaque on the monument in Thorpe, West Virginia honoring
Henry Harman & his sons George and Matthias

He continued to repeat this tactic and gained a little distance from his assailants each time. When he had gained considerable distance, he continued to race without stopping—thinking to outrun them. But while the others lagged behind, there was one fleet warrior, whose speed he could not surpass, who still pressed closely after him. Long and hot was the chase until at length, being so far ahead of the others that he felt sure of being able to dispatch the untiring savage before the others came up, he once more turned and showed him the muzzle of his rifle; al which, the Indian fearing to encounter Henry alone with an empty gun, turned and gave up the chase. The balance of this narrative about the exploits of Henry Harman is reproduced, word for word using the spelling, punctuation and terminology exactly as handwritten by William Neel Harman, grandson of Henry Harman, allowing the true emotions of the participants to be expressed to the reader.

Part 4

Hairbreadth Escapes
Written by John Newton Harman Sr. 1924

Knowing their trails and lurking places, Captain Harman sometimes went alone, as a scout, to discover the approach or whereabouts of the Indians. On one occasion, being on a scout and on foot, he suddenly discovered a large band of them on horseback, coming directly toward him at a point where there seemed no possible way to escape, save by trying to hide himself under some lodged grass beside the path along which they were to pass. Seeing that they had not discovered him, he had barely time to throw himself under the lodged and leaning grass. On they quickly came and rode by, Indian file, so close the horses' hoofs almost trod upon him, but passed without seeing him. Thus, he escaped a frightful death and perhaps torture at their hands.

On another occasion, being on horseback and a number of miles away from the fort, he was waylaid by them, and his large bay mare shot down under and on him. The mare, falling on one of his legs.

Held him fast on the ground. Seeing the savages rushing on him with uplifted tomahawks, and being a man of gigantic strength, he drew up the other foot, placed his heel against the mare's back and by herculean efforts pushed the huge beast off his leg, leaped to his feet rifle in hand, and pointing it at their breasts, made them take trees, and not giving them time to load their empty guns, ran for his life, till seeing them started in pursuit, he again drew his loaded rifle and made them take trees, and again ran for life, till the pack got started after him, when he again drew his rifle and made them take to trees; in this way gaining a little distance from his assailants every time. Having repeated this operation 'till he had gained considerable distance he now continued to race without stopping thinking to outrun them. But while others lagged behind, there was one feet warrior whose speed he could not surpass, who still pressed closely after him. Long and hot was the chase, till at length, being so far ahead of the others, that he felt sure of being able to dispatch this untiring savage before the others came up. he once more showed him the muzzle of his gun; at which, the Indian fearing to encounter him alone. Turned and gave up the chase. And our hero reached the fort in safety.

Part 5

The Battle of Warfield and the Capture of Jane Wily

Of all the heroic feats or hand-to-hand death—grapple encounters with the Indians in the border warfare of this or any country—none surpass the superb achievement of Capt. Henry Harman and his sons at The Battle of the Warfield on Tug River named in honor of that event. It occurred on the 12th of November 1788, Capt. Harman with his sons George & Mathias (18 years old) and George Draper proceeded with thirty packhorses to Tug River to hunt bears and pack home the meat, and finding a suitable point struck camp-staked out their horses and leaving George (Draper) to prepare their supplies the others went hunting. Shortly afterwards George discovered what he took to be the signs of Indians and by a signal recalled his comrades from *The Hunt*. His father examined the signs including a pair of leggings which he smelled and by the smell which he well knew, and possessions and their bag recognized the sign to be of Indians-and from appearances supposed to be about 10 in number.

A council or consultation was at once held, what was best to be done. There were two ways back to the settlements—one a near & direct route up the river—the other a circuitous mountain route by which it would require several days to reach the settlements. It was known that the men of Bluestone & Abbs Valley were all out hunting—the hunting season having arrived & the women and children left defenseless at their homes and certain prey for the blood thirsty savages. Seeing the Indian trail led directly up the river Draper & the two younger Harman's strongly advocated the mountain route, but the old man whose word was law, with an emphatic gesture declared, "I will warn Bluestone this night at the risk of my life". Noble superb, heroic deed! But for this, the Black Wolf, with his band of Shawnee warriors, now directly in the way up the river route-in no wise appeased by many massacres & butcheries he had already made in the 11 years preceding-would have made a perfectly complete holocaust of the women

& children of the Bluestone settlements. The line of march was soon taken directly up the river. Draper rode next to Capt. Harman in front and George & Mathias brought up the rear driving the packhorses. At the shake of every bush Draper would exclaim "here they are". Having twice forded the river and directly after ascending the bank from the second crossing a trained bear dog was sent ahead of the men, and that when the dog reared up on a log behind which the Indians were concealed, that he came running back whining, with his hair turned upward down and carrying his tail tucked between his legs. This action by the dog gave the Harman's a moment in which to dismount before the Indians fired upon them.

Capt. Harman exclaimed "there you lie you sad murdering dogs". They were armed with rifles tomahawks war-clubs, bows and brass-headed arrows. In an instant they rose & fired upon the whites but without effect. But with their terrific war-hoops with which they made the woods resound they now rushed on Capt. Harman with drawn tomahawks expecting in an instant to take his scalp. Draper having at the first fire wheeled his horse and unceremoniously fled. George seeing Draper's flight past him turned his eyes towards his father now half surrounded by his savage assailants and by pointing his loaded gun at them kept them from surrounding him. George heard him call over his shoulder—" good lord, my sons, don't leave me."

George relates that, from that moment he knew no fear-rushed to his father's side and in his eagerness to slay the foremost assailant who proved to be the veritable "wolf his newly Dickert Gun used a little too quick but striking & wounding the savage in the knee. The father's gun—now with deadly aim sent a ball through an Indians heart that fell & expired. The father had taken the precaution to forbid Mathias to shoot & thus kept a loaded gun ready to prevent being tomahawked by the savages—trying to load his gun with his left hand (the Harman's all carried their shot pouches on their left side).

George was struck by an arrow which pierced entirely through the double of his arm and with the other hand he jerked out the barb point foremost from behind next to the shoulder & doing so dropped his ramrod. From this wound the blood spouted freely-being a lame man from white swelling a stout athletic savage seeing him limp and his blood flowing freely deemed him an easy prey. Throwing down his unloaded gun and advancing on George with up lifted tomahawk, but George by a sudden blow with his gun barrel knocked the top of his head & repeatedly threw the Indian to the ground but the Indian being clad in a tight calico hunting shirt, George found it impossible to hold him long enough to reach his butchers knife which in the scuffle still slipped around his back beyond his grasp.

In this life & death struggle so long protracted-George at length-upon throwing his slippery antagonist got his hand upon his knife and plunged it deep in the Indians side. While continuing to do so over again another Indian took in the situation and advanced on George with a war club which he drew steadily over George's head to make a sure lick at that moment there was a sharp crack of a rifle. The father's eye had caught the situation and sent a ball through that Indian. War club flew high in the air and the Indian with a horsed yell escaping felt prostrate on the ground. It was the father's rifle.

Mathias who had now determined to not shoot but have his loaded gun ever ready, about this time obtained leave and taking good aim killed another Indian. George now behind Wolf trying to drag off the wounded Indian towards a thicket of laurel on the bank of the river. He drew his rifle, which he had now loaded and made present but the cunning Wolf bounding first to the one side and then the other gained the thicket. While that was going on an Indian Chief calling himself Cherokee (so stated in the sworn narrative of Mrs. Willy) singled out & approached Capt. Harman (whom he called Skigusti-great warrior) for single combat—approaching up close to him, he drew a deadly arrow, and Harman drew his rifle which he had reloaded.

Both shot or aimed to shoot at the same moment of time. The cock of the gun lock caught half-cock and it failed to fire. The arrow pierced double of Capt. Harman's arm cutting a large blood vessel from which as soon as he jerked out the barbed arrow the blood sprouted. Harman again cocked and drew his gun speedily. The savage drawing another arrow advanced till the arrow and the muzzle of the gun passed each other. The gun again missed fire and the arrow struck a rib of Capt. Harman not the heart which glanced around and was finally cutout behind his shoulder. Thinking he had now killed the Indian jumped behind a sapling as Harman drew his gun for the third time and continued to spring rapidly back & fourth behind the sapling till Harman's gun fired shooting him through the arm near the

21

body—as learned from Mrs. Wily.

Soon afterwards Capt. Harman sunk down & fainted from loss of blood. George returning to his side got water & threw in his face & he revived and said we are not whipped, give me my pipe and while he took a smoke George seeing something glitter in the moon light now shining found it was the bright tomahawk of the Indian, he had killed and scalped. The Indian which scalp is preserved in the family to this day. The Indian Wolf & Cherokee beholding 4 of their numbers slain and made an escape for life. Wolf shot one horse the result made it a cripple for life. The other horse wounded severely of which died that night. The raiders went dragging & supporting their wounded comrade down the warpath where Draper was hiding in a tree-top from which escaping after they had passed.

He took his route by the circuitous mountains south to the settlements where the Harman's had already arrived and finding a concourse of people assembled and beginning to tell them that the Harman's were all killed. It is said hearing it George drew his hunting knife and made at Draper and he had to get away from there. The brass & barbed arrow point being cut out behind Capt. Harman's left shoulder he speedily recovered and lived at his home where we reside now, lived till the fall of the year 1821 with his youngest son (Elias) (the writer's father at which date bloody flux breaking out in the family he with other members of the family died with flux) about one year from the date of the battle.

In the fall of 1789, a band of Indians led by this same Wolf & Cherokee made another raid into the Bluestone settlements and captured Miss Jane (or Jean) Wily and an infant child of hers she being then 9 months of another and carried them down the lower fork of Sandy (River). On the route she became the mother of another child. Whether her husband was killed tradition does not say—no one has noticed or made any record of this event as far as this writer is informed. The property was near the Harman homestead. The Indians carried her to the Harman battleground-Warfield-gathered up the bones of the Indians that died including the one that died the night after the battle, placed them in a hollow log & mourned over them. Pointing out the exact spot where he fought with Captain Harman. Cherokee said, "right there I killed Skigusti", (reckless whether they might kill her Mrs. Wily replied no you didn't for he is now alive & well). He replied you lie, you virginny bitch for when I shot him, he called upon his God". They took (her) further down the river and took her and her children into a cave and tied her feet to stakes driven into the ground then they went out for days to hunt. One day they came in hurriedly and said there were some younackys (meaning white men) seized up her two children & knocked their brains out upon the rocks and ran out—leaving her staked to the ground She now ruffled till she got one hand loose and with it untied the other, and finding herself loose she ran for life toward the river-reaching the bank she hollowed and a man named Adam Harman came to the other bank and hurriedly made a raft of logs, came across and rescued her just as (they) got to the opposite bank they looked back and saw an Italian.

Part 6

Daniel Harman son of Capt. Henry "Old Skygusty" Harman From the annals of Tazewell County, Virginia

Daniel Harman left his house, on the head of Clinch, on a fine morning in the fall of 1791, for the purpose of killing a deer. Where he went for that purpose is not known, but having done so, he started for home, with the deer fastened to the cantle of his saddle.

Harman was a great hunter and owned a choice rifle, remarkable for the beauty of its finish and the superior structure of its triggers, which were, as usual, of the double kind. So strong was the spring of these, that, when sprung, the noise might be heard for a considerable distance. He was riding a large, spirited horse and the lad got within a mile of home, and was passing through a bottom, near the present residence, and on the lands of William O. George, when suddenly a party of Indians sprang from behind a log and fired on him. He was unhurt, and putting spurs to his horse, away he went through the heavy timber, forgetting all other danger, in his precarious situation.

On he went, but his horse, passing too near a tree, struck the rider's knee, breaking his leg and throwing him from his horse. In a few minutes the savages were upon him, and, with their tomahawks, soon put an end to his sufferings. The horse continued his flight 'till he got to the house, at which were several of the neighbors, who immediately went to look after Harman. Passing near the Indians they heard the click of Harman's well-known trigger. A panic struck the men, and running in zigzag lines, they made a rapid retreat, leaving the Indians to silently retrace their steps from the settlement.

Part 7

Mathias "Tice" Harman
The Founding of Harman's Station

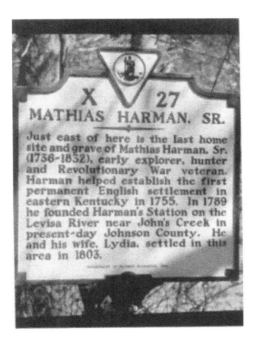

athias Harman was called "Tice" or "Tias" Harman by his companions. He was diminutive in size, in height being but little more than five feet, and his weight never exceeded one hundred and twenty pounds. He had an enormous nose and a thin sharp face. He had an abundance of hair of a yellow tinge, beard of a darker hue, blue eyes which anger made green and glittering, and a bearing bold and fearless. He possessed an iron constitution and could endure more fatigue and privation than any of his associates. He was a dead shot with the long rifle of his day. The Indians believed him in league with the devil or some other malevolent power because of their numbers he killed, his miraculous escapes, and the bitterness and relentless daring of his warfare against them. He was one of the Long Hunters, as were others of the Harman's, and more than once did his journeys into the wilderness carry him to the Mississippi River. He and the other Harman's able to bear arms were in the Virginia service in the War of the Revolution. He is said to have formed the colony which made the first settlement in Ab's Valley. He formed the colony which made the first settlement in Eastern Kentucky and erected the blockhouse. He brought in the settlers who rebuilt the blockhouse, and for a number of years he lived in the Blockhouse bottom or its vicinity. In his extreme old age, he returned to Virginia and died there. It is said he lived to be ninety-six, but I have not the date or place of his death.

"Written by WILLIAM ELSEY CONNELLEY,
New York, New York Torch Press 1910

From Eagle Oak and Other Poems,
by Captain Samuel H. Newbery

Come. turn your eyes toward the East,
If would enjoy a muse's feast;
Follow yon mountain's line of blue
'Till High Rock's brow shall greet your view;
Who lifts his head above the vale
Where sleeps the hero of my tale.
Whose gallant sons beside him stood
In the mountainous solitude.

Their story brief though coming late.
In simple verse I will relate.
Skyduskee with his daring sons.
With horses packed and rifle guns;
George Draper too who went along,
Must be remembered in my song.
In search of game one autumn day.
They took their journey far away.

Perhaps a hundred miles or so,
To where Tug river's waters flow.
The beechen mast was coming down.
And bears were plenty all around.
So, when they reached their camping ground,
The sons were sent to search around
To see if any "Injun Sign"
Might be found along the line

Where they proposed their camp to make,
To roast or fry their venison steak;
If favored luck should grant their aim
And help them to their fancied game,
That each pack horse might have a load

To bear o'er hills without a road.
Skyduskee's sons, in searching around,
Soon found some Red Men's camping ground,
Where they had spent the night before,
And cooked and ate their meagre store.

The burning brands were scarcely cold,
Their present danyer plainly told;
Then, hurrying back to camp, they found,
Their horses hoppled all around,
Who to their father made report?
With all the facts to give support.
Skrduskee was a woodsman born,
In danger reared—all fear to scorn,
Nor reckless in life's battlefield,
But prudent to no foeman yield.

The vantage ground when life's the stake,
If duty did precaution take:
As life was not a useless gift,
Though Red Men claimed the right to lift
The scaly from any human head
Even before the scalped was dead.
Soon the horses were all repacked,
To make for home before attacked;
No time to parley, or to wait.
"It was action then, and not debate.

Their safety was in quick retreat,
But in good order and complete;
The older ones in front appear,
The Harman sons to be in the rear.
The silent march was then begun—
Each hunter with his loaded gun.
While every eye was wide awake,

As looking for some poison snake,
The sullen Indian in his wrath
Was crouched along his narrow path.

Six in number, behind a log,
Out of the sight of man or dog:
Two had bows and arrows strong
Four had rifles near five feet long;
Had they but known their weapons, worth
They'd wiped the Harman's from the earth.
When at the signal of their chief
The awful silence found relief;
Four rifle balls went whizzing out
And followed close by savage shout.

Bad luck to them—their aim had missed
Four bullets through the air had hissed.
The Harman's formed in hollow square,
But Draper was no longer there—
His horse had born him far away,
Out of reach of the bloody fray.
Skrduskee and his oldest son
Each to his shoulder found his gun,
And quick as thought-with truest aim—
Indians two were limping lame.

Their combs were out by Harman's gaffs
That made them squirm and devil's laugh;
The others then, in maddened strife,
With tomahawks and scalping knife
Around the three were closing in
To put an end to all the din.
But soon they found a loaded gun.
Was leveled by the youngest son,
Who at his father's wise request.

Had kept it to his bosom pressed

With seeming aim, he watched the fray,
And kept the savages at bay;
While father and the older son
We're sending death from smoking gun,
And he above with watchful eye,
Could hear the deathly missiles Ay.
'The time for him to act was near.
He saw the chieftain's form appear.
So, anxious he, to try his luck
As well to test his nerve and pluck.

Permission asked from father nearby,
Who gave it with a hearty cheer?
On wings of death a bullet flew,
That pierced the Shawnee chieftain through,
Who fell beneath a tall beech tree,
With daring spirit—forever free.
The older son, to tell the truth,
He had been lamed from early youth;
His foeman saw him limping 'round,
Vis took his lameness for a wound.

And rushing on him for his scalp—
As well might he attack the Alps.
Though George was lame, he found him tough and wiry too—
as well as rough—A rough and tumble fight begun,
Without the aid of any gun.
George Harman's knife was in his belt,
Although for it he'd often felt;
With ease, he threw the Red Man down,
But could not hold him on the ground,
His shot pouch on his left side hung,
In his tussle to his back was slung.

In vain he sought his truant knife,
To put an end to the Red Man's life,
Though failing oft, the time came 'round,
And found him dead on the battle ground.
"It was hand to hand-and tilt for tilt,
Until the Red Man's blood was spilt.
Whose scalping knife had turned that day,
And to his heart had carved its way;
Whose ghost went out where the knife went in,
Stained with the blood of a brother's sin.

'Twas life for life, the grace that's paid
By all who join in be horrid trade—
Savage civilized—me and all—
The strongest rise, the weakest fall.
Mathias and George had done good work;
None but Draper had seemed to shirk;
Four out of six were put to rest.
The other two, their father pressed
With arrows flying from the bow.
Till blood began to freely flow.

Whose nerve and pluck were of the best,
One arrow fastened in his breast.
Who seeing that their chief was dead?
Became disheartened, turned and fled.
As through the forest on they sped.
Perhaps not mindful of their dead.
Though twice their number lost or killed;
Their beating hearts forever stilled;
Without a scalp on either belt.
Their woeful luck they keenly felt.

The battle o'er the day was won.
By Henry and his worthy sons.

Though two to one had been the odds—
The brave are aided by the gods.
With willing hand and willing heart,
Half the battle is in the start.
The aim of justice is the right,
Though not always in the fight;
But courage is the god of will
Whose purpose is to rule or kill.

The time of fight had passed away—
To dress the wounded in the fray,
To get the arrow from the breast
Of their father, was then the test.
The headed arrowhead was flared—
And bleeding bosom must be bared
To get the horrid weapon out,
Though followed by a bloody spout.
With pocketknife then cut it loose,
Then worked away the gory sluice.

Then bound it up as best they could—
Determined, then, to leave the wood,
And leave the wilds and wilder still
The Red man with his stubborn will;
With tomahawk and scalping knife,
Who had pledged his sacred life
To save his father's hunting ground,
Where trespassers were often found;
Which pledge he kept with bloody hand
'Till driven from his father's land.

The homeward march was soon begun—
Brave Henry with his valiant sons,
Though somewhat damaged in the fight,
But living foes all put to flight:

Full conscious of their duty done
With hunting knife and trusty gun,
Although their horses bore no packs,
But empty all, and going back,
They'd left their home in search of game,
Returning then—with naught but fame.

The Harman's were of warrior clan—
Their sires came from the Isle of Man.
Skyduskee was of massive frame—
The Red Man gave to him his name
Because he was of stately form,
Both tall and straight-a soldier born,
With darkened brows and flashing eye,
From dangers form would never fy;
Whose motto was: To never vield
Till every foeman quit the field.

Rather than show the feather white.
Would sink his name in endless night.
I've often seen their battle ground
And fancied I could hear the sound
Of whizzing balls and twanging bows
Between the Elermans and their focus;
Or faintly bear the raven's croak
Amid the bwanches of the oak.
And Aying ruitures from afar—
The filthy scavengers of war.

All, it schemed had heard the groans,
And swiftly came to pick the bones.
Year sis score years have rolled away
With rifle gun and date of strife.
Since that fearful autumn day;
An Indian and hunting knife.

Were carved upon the bole of beech.
As high as carving hand could reach.
That noted beech no more appears,
Although it stood a hundred years.

The sacrilegious hand of man
Has marred the spot where savage clan
Once dared to lift his feeble hand
In the defense of native land:
With erring judgment staking all.
And saw his sylvan empire fall.

Chapter 3

*The Capture and Rescue of Mrs. Ingles
('Taken from Trans-Alleghany Pioneers.)*
Mrs. Ingles rescued by Adam Harman and his two sons.

William Ingles and Mary Draper were married in 1750. This was the first white wedding west of the Alleghany. On the 8th of July, 1755, being Sunday and the day before Braddock's memorable defeat, near Fort Du Quesne, when all was peace and there was no suspicion of harm or danger, a party of Shawnees from beyond the Ohio River fell upon the Draper's Meadows settlement and killed, wounded, or captured every soul there present. as follows: Col. James Patton, Mrs. George Draper, Casper Barrier, and a child of John Draper were killed; Mrs. John Draper was James Cull. wounded: Mrs. William Ingles, Mrs. John Draper, and Henry Leonard. Prisoners. The Indians traveled down the New River with their captives and reached the capitol town of the Shawnees, at the mouth of the Scioto River, just one month after leaving the scene of the massacre and capture of Draper's Meadows.

Soon after their arrival at the Indian town, the prisoners were all separated and allotted to different owners. and not again allowed to see or communicate with each other. The only other white female in the camp was an elderly Dutch woman who had been captured in Western Pennsylvania. Mrs. Ingles succeeded in persuading her to join her escape.

Supplied with one blanket each, they started late in the afternoon on their perilous journey. Day after day they dragged their weary limbs along, suffering and starving; night after night they shivered, starved, and suffered, crawling into hollow logs or hollow trees as partial protection from the increasing cold, and thus they traversed this now beautiful valley, then an unbroken wilderness, never penetrated by the foot of a white person until Mrs. Ingles and others passed through it a few months before as prisoners.

When the fugitives were passing near the mouth of the East River, at the future point of the New River Division, of the Norfolk and Western Railroad where it now leaves New River, the old woman became desperate, and this time more dangerous than ever. In the extremity of her suffering from starvation and exhaustion, she threatened to kill Mrs. Ingles with cannibalistic intent.

Mrs. Ingles tried temporizing by proposing to "draw cuts" to determine which one should be the victim; the old woman consented to this. The lot fell to Mrs. Ingles; she then appealed to the old woman's cupidity by offering her large rewards when they got home if she would spare her; but the pangs of present hunger were more potent than the hope of future gain, and she undertook, then and there, to immolate her victim.

She succeeded in getting Mrs. Ingles in her grasp, and it became a struggle for life or death. How sad that these poor women, after all they had suffered and endured together, should now, in that vast solitude, alone, with no eve to see, nor hand to save or aid, be engaged in a hand-to-hand, life-or-death struggle: the old woman, to prevent death by starvation, would kill her companion for food, while Mrs. Ingles was trying to save her life from the murderous hand of her companion, probably to die a lingering death from starvation; the choice seemed worth but little. If they had more strength, the result might have been more serious, or possibly fatal, to one or both.

But both were so feeble that neither had done the other much hurt until Mrs. Ingles, being much the younger (she was then but 28), and by comparison still somewhat more active, succeeded in escaping from the clutches of her adversary and started on up the river, leaving the old woman greatly exhausted by the struggle. When well out of sight, she slipped under the river bank and secreted herself until the old woman had recovered breath and passed on, supposing that Mrs. Ingles was still in advance.

This scene occurred late in the evening, between sundown and darkness. When Mrs. Ingles emerged from her concealment, the moon was up and shining brightly, and by its light, she discovered, near at hand, a canoe at the river bank, half full of leaves, blown into it by the wind, but there was no paddle, oar, or pole; as a substitute, she picked up, after some search, a small slab or sliver from a shattered tree, blown down by a storm.

36

She had never before undertaken literally to "paddle her own canoe" and found much difficulty at first in guiding it, but. per serving patiently, she caught the knack of steering it, and as the river was low and not much current at the place, she succeeded in making her way safely across.

Here, to her great relief, she found a cabin or camp that had been built by some hunters from the settlements above and a patch where they had attempted to raise some corn. Seeing no one about the place being deserted she crept into the cabin and spent the night. The next morning, she searched the patch for some corn, but was sadly disappointed to find that the buffalo, bears, and other wild animals had utterly destroyed it; she discovered it in the ground however, two small turnips which the animals had failed to find and on these, she made a sumptuous breakfast.

Resuming her now solitary journey, she had gone but a short distance when she discovered her late companion on the opposite shore. They halted and held a parley. The old woman professed great remorse and penitence. and made all sorts of fair promises for the future. and begged piteously to be brought over, or that Mrs. Ingles would come back to her, that they might continue their journey together. With Mrs. Ingles, it was a question between sympathy and safety but a wise discretion prevailed. After all that had occurred, she concluded that it would be safer to keep the river between them, and, accordingly, each went her way on opposite sides.

MRS. INGLES ARRIVAL AT EGGLESTON SPRINGS.

Mrs. Ingles, after getting to the bottom of the cliff, had gone but a short distance when to her joyful surprise she discovered, just before her, a patch of corn. She approached it as rapidly as she could moving her painful limbs along. She saw no one but there were evident signs of persons about. She hallooed, at first there was no response, but relief was near at hand. She was about to be saved, and just in time. She had been heard by Adam Harman and his two sons, whose patch it was and who were in it gathering their corn. Suspecting upon hearing a voice that there might be an intended attack by Indians, they grabbed their rifles, always kept close at hand, and listened attentively.

Mrs. Ingles hollered again, they came out from the corn and towards her, cautiously rifles in hand. When near enough to distinguish the voice

Mrs. Ingles still hallooing Adam Harman remarked to his sons: "Surely that must be Mrs. Ingles' voice." Just then she too recognized Harman, when she was overwhelmed with emotions of joy and relief poor, overtaxed nature gave way and she swooned and fell, insensible, to the ground. They picked her up tenderly and conveyed her to their little hut near at hand where there was protection from the storm; a reusing fire and substantial comfort.

Mrs. Ingles soon revived, and the Harman's were unremitting in their kind attention and efforts to promote her comfort. They had in their cabin a stock of fresh venison and bear meat; they set to work to cook and make a soup of some of this, and with excellent judgment would permit their patient to take but little at a time in her famished condition.

While answering her hurried questions as to what they knew about her home and friends, they warmed some water in their skillet and bathed her still and swollen feet and limbs, after which they wrapped her in their blankets and stowed her away tenderly on their pallet in the corner which to her, by comparison, was "soft as downy pillows are", and a degree of luxury she had not experienced since she was torn from her own home by ruthless savages more than four months before. Under these new and favoring conditions of safety and comfort, it is no wonder that "nature's sweet restorer" soon came to her relief and bathed her wearied senses and aching limbs in balmy restful, and refreshing sleep.

Mrs. Ingles had not seen a fire for forty days (since leaving Big Bone Lick); she had not tasted food, except nuts, corn, and berries, for forty days; she had not known shelter, except caves or hollow logs or deserted camps, for forty days; she had not known a bed, except the bare earth, or leaves or moss, for forty days. She had been constantly exposed to the danger of recapture and death by the savages, danger from wild beasts, sickness, accident, exposure and starvation, and danger from her companion. Yet, notwithstanding all these, she had within these forty days run, walked, crawled, climbed, and waded seven or eight hundred miles including detours up and down the streams, through a howling wilderness, and was saved at last.

Dr. Tanner's forty days fast the conditions, and circumstances considered, dwindles into insignificance compared with this. Indeed, I do not know, in all history, the record of a more wonderful and heroic performance than that of this brave little woman, all things considered. It is said to be as heroic to endure as to dare; then Mrs. Ingles was doubly heroic, for she dared and endured all, that humans can.

The "immortal "Six Hundred" who "rode into the gates of death and the jaws of hell" were soldiers under military discipline. When commanded, they knew only to obey; they were accustomed to deeds of daring and death. They knew their duty and they did it grandly, nobly, heroically. When ordered to charge, they nerved themselves for the shock, which could last but a few minutes. Death might come to them within these few minutes; indeed, it probably would; but if it came, it would be sudden and almost painless and if they escaped, the strain would soon be over, and glory awaited them.

Not so with Mrs. Ingles. This delicate woman, reared in comfort and ease, and unaccustomed to hardships, being in the hands of savages, in a vast wilderness, beyond civilization and beyond human aid, coolly and deliberately resolved to attempt her escape knowing that the odds were overwhelming against her; knowing that if recaptured, she would suffer death by torture, and if she escaped recapture it would probably be to suffer a lingering death by exposure, fatigue and starvation; but her resolution was fixed; she nerved herself, not for the struggle of a few minutes only, but they were strung to a tension that must be sustained at the highest pitch, by heroic fortitude, for weeks, possibly for months of mental anxiety and physical suffering, whether she finally escaped or perished.

But, to return to the Harman cabin. Mrs. Ingles awoke the next morning, greatly rested and refreshed. She called Mr. Harman and told him of her experience with the old woman, her companion, and begged him to send his boys back down the river in search of her, but the boys, having heard Mrs. Ingles relate the story of her adventure with the old woman, and very naturally, feeling outraged and indignant at her conduct, refused to go, and Harman, sharing their feelings, declined to compel them; so, the old woman was left for the present, to make her own way as best she could.

Harman and his sons had been neighbors of Mrs. Ingles at Draper's Meadows before her capture and before they came down here to make their new clearing and settlement. As neighbors on a frontier where neighbors are scarce, they had known each other well. Harman considered no attention, labor or pains too, great to testify his friendship for Mrs. Ingles and tender regard for her distressed condition. He had brought to this new camp when he came, two horses and a few cattle to range on the rich wild pea vine, which grew here luxuriantly.

He had heard in his time, and it impressed itself upon his memory that beef tea was the best of all nourishing and strengthening diets and restoratives for persons in a famished and exhausted condition; so, although he had as before stated, plenty of nice, fresh game meat in his cabin he took his rifle, and, against the protests of Mrs. Ingles went out hunted up and shot down a nice fat beef to get a little piece as big as his hand, to boil in his tin cup, to make her some beef tea and make it he did, feeding her, first with the tea alone, and then with tea and beef, until, within a couple of days.

Thanks to her naturally robust constitution and health, she was sufficiently recovered, rested and strengthened to travel; when he put her on one of his horses himself taking the other, and started with her to her home at Draper's Meadows some ten or twelve miles distant up the river, but when they arrived at the settlement there was an Indian alarm and all the neighbors had congregated at a fort at "Dunkard Bottom" on the west side of the river, a short distance above "Ingles' Ferry," so they went on to this place, arriving about night and Mrs. Ingles had with glad surprise a joyful meeting with such of her friends as were present in the fort. The next morning after arriving at the fort, Mrs. Ingles again begged Harman, now that he had restored her to her friends, to comfort and safety, to go back and hunt for the poor old woman, and if she's still alive, to bring her in. This he now consented to do and started promptly down the west bank of the river.

On the other hand, a few minutes after the old woman and Mrs. Ingles had parted company, the old woman met with a genuine piece of good luck. She came upon a hunter's camp, just abandoned apparently precipitately, for what reason she could not tell--possibly from an Indian alarm-but they had left on the fire a kettle of meat cooking, to which she addressed herself assiduously. She remained here for two or three days, resting, eating, and recuperating her strength.

The hunters had left at the camp an old pair of leather breeches; the old woman appropriated to her own personal use and adornment, being by no means fastidious about the fit, or the latest style of fashion, her own

40

clothes being almost entirely gone. An old horse had also been left by the supposed hunters, loose about the camp, but no sign of saddle or bridle. The old woman remained at the camp its sole occupant (no one putting in an appearance while she was there until she had consumed all the meat in the pot; she then made a sort of bridle or halter of leatherwood bark, caught the old horse, put on him that same bell which was found on the horse, captured opposite Scioto, and taken off by the practical-minded old woman when that horse had been abandoned to his fate among the drift logs in Big Sandy and carried through all her terrible struggles and suffering to this place.

Having taken the wrapper from around the clapper and so hung the bell on the horse's neck that it would tinkle as he went, as being so near the settlement, she now hoped to meet settlers or hunters, she mounted him, riding in the style best adapted to her newly-acquired dress of leather unmentionables, and again started up the river on her way to the then frontier settlement. Thus, slowly jogging along, hallooing from time to time to attract the attention of anyone who might be within hearing she was met in this plight, about the "Horse Shoe," or mouth of Back Creek, opposite "Buchannan's Bottom," by Adam Harman, in search of her, and taken on to the fort.

The meeting between Mrs. Ingles and the old woman was very affecting. Their last parting had been in a hand-to-hand struggle for life or death not instigated by malice or vindictiveness, but by that first great law of nature, self-preservation that recognizes no human law but now that they were both saved, this little episode was tacitly considered as forgotten. Remembering only the common dangers they had braved and the common sufferings they had endured together in the inhospitable wilderness they fell upon each other's necks and wept, and all was reconciliation and peace. The old woman remained here for a time awaiting an opportunity to get to her own home and friends in Pennsylvania.

Finding before long an opportunity of getting as far as Winchester by wagon she availed herself of it and from there with her precious bell the sole trophy of her terrible travels and travails, it was hoped and believed that she soon got safely home, though I cannot learn that she was ever afterward heard of in the New River settlement. I regret that not even her name has been preserved. In the traditions of the Ingles family, she is known and remembered only as "the old Dutch woman.

Adam Harman having accomplished his mission of mercy and improved the unexpected opportunity of a social reunion with his late neighbors and friends, took an affectionate leave of Mrs. Ingles and her friends and returned to his new camp down the river. This settlement of Harman's was at a point on the east bank of New River and is now the Site of that well known place of summer resort the "New River White Sulphur", "Chapman's." or "Eggleston's Springs." which for grandeur and beauty of scenery, is probably not excelled by any of the beautiful watering places of the Virginia mountains. The New River branch of the Norfolk and Western Railroad runs along the opposite shore of the river, the station for this place being called "Ripplemead."

The formidable cliff described above, the climbing over which occupied Mrs. Ingles one whole day, the most terrible of her life, is immediately below the springs, is a part of the spring's estate, and well known to the frequenters of that popular resort. The little core immediately above the cliff, and then site of the Harman cabin and corn patch, is now, as I am informed, called "Clover Nook." I regret that I do not know the after-history of Adam Harman and his sons the pioneer settlers of this beautiful place; but from every descendant of Mrs. Ingles, now and forever, I bespeak proper appreciation and grateful remembrance of the brave tender-hearted, sympathetic, noble Adam Harman. Twenty or thirty years later there was a family of Harman's-Henry and his sons, George and Matthias who distinguished themselves for their coolness and bravery as Indian fighters in the Clinch settlements of Tazewell.

I presume they were of the same Harman stock, but just what relations to Adam I do not know. I stated above that Mrs. Ingles on her arrival at the fort, had a joyful meeting with such of her friends as she found there; but the two of all others whom she had hoped and expected to find there --the two for whom her heart had yearned with deepest love, and the hope again of seeing whom had sustained her in her captivity and nursed her to her desperate exertions in her escape, her husband and her brother--were not there. They had gone, some weeks before, down to the Cherokee Nation in the Tennessee and Georgia region to see if they could get any tidings of their lost families and, if so, to try, through the Cherokees they then being friendly with the whites and also with the Indian tribes north of the Ohio River, to ransom and recover them; but their expedition had been fruitless, and they were returning sad, disconsolate, despairing, almost hopeless.

On the night that Mrs. Ingles had reached the fort, William Ingles and John Draper stayed within a few miles of it, and about where the town of Newbern Pulaski County now stands. Next morning, they made a daylight start and arrived at the fort to breakfast, and to find, to their inexpressible joy and surprise, that Mrs. Ingles had arrived the night before. Such a meeting, under such circumstances, and after all that had occurred since they last parted, nearly five months before, may be imagined, but cannot be described. I shall not attempt it. There is probably no happiness in this life without alloys, no sweet without its bitter; no rose without its thorn. Though William and Mary Ingles were inexpressibly rejoiced to be restored to each other, their happiness was saddened by the bitter thought that their helpless little children were still in the hands of savages; and while John Draper was overjoyed to have his sister return, he could not banish the ever-present and harrowing thought that his wife was still in the far-off wilderness--in the hands of savages and her fate unknown".

Chapter 4

The Harman/Harmon Legacy Continued
August 1844

While young Peter Harman traveled down the worn-out road to Mary Creekmore's home, he felt his heart pounding as loud as the clomping of his horse's hooves. Would Mary agree to be his bride? Would her father consent to their union? For days, he rehearsed in his head what he would say. True, he was a farmer, but he had saved what he could to show Mr. Creekmore that he could provide a life for his daughter. He would promise that this was just the beginning, that he would continue to provide for Mary. He would detail for her father, that he would work hard for her. This brown haired, soft-spoken woman consumed his thoughts. He wanted to spend the rest of his life with her. Mary shared his dream and longed for the day that she would be Mrs. Peter Harman.

"Whoa!" He called out to his horse as he came to a stop in front of Mary's home. Beads of sweat trickled down his cheeks. What would he do if her father did not give his consent? He did not have a backup plan, just a nervous pit in his stomach. He whispered a silent prayer along the way that everything would work out and that he would leave the Creekmore farm with Mary as his fiancée. With hat in hand, he collected his thoughts and knocked on the door. He visited Mary at her home several times before under the watchful eye of her mother. He was careful not to stay longer than 15 minutes on each visit. While he courted Mary, he gave her gifts of freshly picked flowers, chocolates, and two books that he bought for a nickel at the general store. The two met at church, country fairs, and picnics. Peter always treated Mary like a lady. Always a gentleman, he pulled her chair out for her, helped her put her coat on, held the door open for her, offered his seat to her, and always walked her to the door at the end of their dates. When they walked down the streets together, he stayed on the outside of the sidewalk, for as a gentleman, it was his duty to protect her from horses and donkeys that would kick up dirt as they passed by or on rainy days when they would splash in puddles. After courtship, marriage was the next step for a couple.

During this time in history, couples dated for a short time before transitioning into married life. Men believed that if they waited too long, then someone else would swoop in and steal the heart of the one they loved before they had a chance to propose. After all, the sole purpose of courtship was to find someone to marry. Still, men and women were selective in whom they chose, remembering that marriage could only end in death. If Mary had changed her mind later, she would have to beg Peter to release her from the marriage. And in most cases, the answer was no. Marriage was seen as more than two people uniting, but as two families coming together as one. So, when selecting a partner, it was taken into consideration how the families would mesh together. Peter had thought of all of that. From the start, he felt that Mary was the one for him. Peter only waited for two days after they met before asking for consent to call on her. Now here he was, five months later, standing before her parents and asking for Mary's hand in marriage. He explained how he loved Mary, how he would provide for her, to make her happy and to give her a fantastic start to a new life together. Mary's parents chimed in with advice for the two of them, and there it was— the couple received their blessing. Peter and Mary were to be married.

The first thing for Peter and Mary's parents to do was to announce their wedding in a church. The Reverend would counsel them on what society would expect of them as husband and wife. Friends, family, and neighbors passed on nuggets of advice as to how to treat each other and of their duties in the home. It seemed like not a day went by that one of the women in town was stopping by to give Mary some marital advice. Ladies reminded Mary of the importance of gardening and preserving food. They gave her lessons on sewing and baking. Most of those things she already knew. Respectfully, she did not tell them that. She merely soaked in their wisdom, knowing that one day she would be the one to give another young bride-to-be marital advice. Peter, too, was taken aside quite often by other townsmen who wanted to give their opinions on the role of husband. They also watched his sharply as he worked on the farm. They tried to keep him educated on the life of a farmer. It was a hard job that required the use of heavy and dangerous equipment. One slip could cause Peter to lose his fingers, or worse, his life.

Peter and Mary wed at her family home on Thursday, November 14, 1844. Peter's parents, Jacob and Mary Shelly Harman, were in attendance, along with his brothers and sisters: Jeremiah, Nathan, Jane, John, Elizabeth, Sarah, Valentine, Jacob, and Mary.

As Mary Creekmore prepared to become Mary Harman, she dressed in a pastel-colored dress with a blue garter belt underneath. Like most brides at that time, she followed the tradition of—Something Old, Something New, Something Borrowed, Something Blue, and a Sixpence in her Shoe. As the two took their vows before their families, the community, and the eyes of God, Mary could not help but wonder what the future held for them. Would they indeed be married 'til death do they part?' Would they have children? How big would their new family grow? How many years would the 'Harman' name carry on for? It was on this day that the Harman family was about to grow—larger than Peter and Mary could ever imagine!

Peter followed through with his promise and built an adorable log home for Mary. The house had real wood floors and glass windows, instead of wooden shutters that were often blown open during storms or by the heavy winter winds. The roof was sturdy as not to allow snow and rain to seep through, like the homes they lived in growing up. Six months later, Mary happily told Peter that she was pregnant. They were both excited to welcome their first baby into the world. Peter carved a cradle for the new baby that they kept at the foot of the bed. She prepared to give birth at home with the assistance of a Rabbit Catcher (Midwife) and the town doctor.

She just tilled the soil for her garden when she learned that she was pregnant. Since the vegetables had yet to start growing, she had time to expand her garden. The fact that a new baby was on the way meant that her family would develop before the first harvest, and she needed to prepare. Her garden was necessary to provide enough food to last her family all year. So, the details of her garden were planned out carefully. She knew which vegetables to plant first as well as how many of each vegetable to include. Mary also considered how well the food preserved once it was jarred and frozen.

The first vegetable to be planted in the ground was salsify. This veggie would stay planted all summer. They could harvest after the first frost. Salsify looked like parsnips but was thinner. They were coarse in texture and tan in color but once peeled, they looked snowy white. They were nicknamed the Oyster Plant because they left an aftertaste of oysters. The problem was that they did not store well. They were preserved in water with lemon juice and eaten fresh. They picked off the long blades of grass that sprouted off the ends of salsify. They cooked them in butter. The tomato plants were stored in the root cellar to grow. They were brought outside at the end of May. While she was planting her tomatoes, Peter would begin the process of increasing his corn crops on the farm. Their peak months were August and September.

To begin planting the corn, first, the ground was plowed, then a horse-drawn marker was used to make grooves in the soil as a guideline. The rows were approximately 3 feet apart, and the seeds spaced 10"-12" apart. The horses were trained to follow verbal commands. "Gee" and a light tug meant a move to the right. "Haw" meant a move to the left. Peter harvested the corn crops on Wednesdays and Fridays. It was cut down with a corn knife that was 2' long and razor sharp. They were put in 100-pound feed bags— five dozen to a bag.

Peter and Mary made hotbeds for the tomato plants. After Mary laid the dirt in the hotbed, she spread cow manure on top, using her bare hands. She then transferred the tomato plants to the hotbed. Straw as thick as 4 inches was spread out around the plants to conserve the moisture and prevent weed growth.

The family used some of the tomatoes. They also sold plants in 8-quart baskets. A bag of corn sold for $1, and the tomatoes were sold for 25–35 cents each. The vegetables not sold were fed to the cows and hogs. A large part of the garden included greens and peas. There were several ways to cook green beans. One idea was to have them simmer in a pot all day with bacon. Then Mary added potatoes, okra, and chunks of corn to make a stew. When she prepared the green beans with other types of meat, she saved the juice for later. The sauce was called pot likker and was either used with soups or poured over toast or biscuits.

Carrots, potatoes, turnips, and cabbage were also planted but not as plentiful since the seeds could be challenging to come by. At the end of summer, a few of those plants would be uprooted and stored in pots in the root cellar to preserve their seeds for the following year. She also had rows of potted vegetables that she continued to grow in the root cellar during the winter months; this included lettuce, kale, spinach, and brussels sprouts. This is how 'root cellars' got their name. As Mary's family grew, so would her garden. An acre of the garden could feed a family of six–eight people.

It was on Thursday, February 19, 1846, that Peter and Mary's first child, Kendrick "KC" Cornelius Harman was born. In Mary's eyes, they were now truly a family.

Every morning, Mary donned herself in the apron that her mother made for her. It was a gift to her on her wedding day. In Mary's eyes, this was one of her most useful items from among of all her possessions. She carried eggs, seeds, and vegetables in the pockets. She used the apron to wipe her hands off and to clean the baby's face. She also used it to protect her hands when she grabbed the oven door or hot pans of food. There was a sleeve on the backside of the apron that was used to carry a rifle. Mary was a lady— but a lady who could shoot a rifle like a man, should she ever encounter wild animals or people looking for trouble. Most importantly, her apron protected her dress underneath from getting stained while she worked in the garden, fed the animals, and cleaned the fireplace. Mary owned only three dresses. One was her good dress and only worn on Sundays and holidays. The cost of fabric was high, so making a new dress was not always an option. Though she typically wore the same dress every day, she would only wash it once a week. She cleaned her apron 2—3 times a week.

She used the burlap sacks from the flour to make clothes for KC. Extra pieces of fabric were used for quilts, pillowcases (at the time they were called pillow slips), and for patches to cover holes in her apron. Companies were soon onto what the ladies were doing and started making burlap sacks with printed patterns for them.

It was soon time to replant the garden. KC stayed by her side in a basket. When he was fussy, she carried KC in a wrap across her chest, so her hands were still free to work. There was no time to stop. She had to keep a constant eye on the insects invading her garden. Certain insects could ravage her garden in days and leave a path of destruction that would render her garden useless. The biggest insect culprit were the locusts.

Though Mary did work long hard hours every day, this did not take away from what Peter endured on the farm. His day started before the sun came up and did not end until the sunset. A farmer's job was backbreaking and more difficult than anyone could imagine. Working under the weight of the heat for hours would often have him drenched in sweat by noon. He allowed himself to take an occasional water break, only to stop from passing out from heat stroke. His body ached at the end of the day, but this was all a part of being a farmer. In his mind, it was all in his duties as husband and father. So, no matter how much it hurt, he never complained. Unfortunately, he suffered from arthritis throughout his body by the time he was 40 years old.

Harvesting crops went on all year. Peter planted barley in February and the oats in early May. He waited until the last day of May before he planted the remaining crops. He knew that by then they were out of danger of another frost passing through the area. He also grew alfalfa hay to feed to the cows and sheep. It was stored in the cow barn and unloaded with a pitchfork. It took up to several hours to finish that job.

Wheat was planted in September and not harvested until the following July or early August. Planting crops in the winter was more difficult since the ground was always frozen. To fight the ice and grow the crops on time, Peter worked together with the neighbors to help each other. Mary and Peter swapped seeds with the neighbors, as well.

Farming equipment was gradually improving and Kentucky farmers, like Peter, were happy with the changes. John Deere now made steel plow blades that replaced the cast iron blades that Peter used as a boy on his family farm. The steel plow blades made it easier to turn the wet soil. This was the first year that Peter was going to try using the mechanical reaper. He had seen it used by other farmers and witnessed how well it worked for them. The mechanical reaper replaced the scythe. Reaping (cutting) the crops was a painstaking task done by hand, with the scythe, a long-curved blade attached to a long pole. However, the mechanical reaper, which was pulled by horses, cut the time and work of reaping almost in half, enabling Peter to plant more crops. With the mechanical reaper, Peter, could cut, thresh, and bundle grain all in one swoop.

There were always jobs at home for Peter. These jobs were mainly taken care of on rainy or snowy days. On those days, he could be found mending fences around the cows and sheep, making repairs to the water well, the family house, the barn and even the outhouse, as needed. For the fence posts, he always used locust posts. They were hand cut from black locust trees. Eighty years later, the locust posts could still be found standing firm while the fence around it crumbled from age and the elements of weather. He also had to grease wagon wheels, oil machinery, and maintain farm equipment.

Not a minute of daylight was ever wasted. Peter woke up on many days before the sun was in the sky. The animals even ate breakfast before Peter did. It was vital that they were fed regularly every day. Milking also had to be done at the same time every day and again at night and in the same order. If this changed even once, the cow's milk production would fall drastically. When he was finally able to sit down for breakfast, it usually included eggs and toast, or porridge.

Occasionally, he had hotcakes made with wheat flour. Horses were a commodity to farmers, and Peter was most certainly appreciative of his horses. He tended to them carefully, making sure to reset the horseshoes or add new shoes when the time came. Each horse harness would be cleaned and repaired regularly. Horses were needed for farm work and were the principal source of travel. They hauled the family's wagon for trips to the general store to trade and barter food, candles, and fabric. If Peter ever needed a new horse, it would cost him half a year's wages. Horses also helped the community as a whole, after blizzards. During some of the more severe snowstorms, up to 300 feet of a road could be blocked off due to snow drifts that would reach up to 4' -6' high. Some of the men and children took to shoveling the way clear. After they removed enough snow, a team of horses rode through to smooth the surface. It wasn't always Peter's horses that were used for the daunting task, though, since the farmers did take turns using their teams.

At county fairs, Peter raced his horses against other farmers'. Horse-racing was a favorite recreation for many people in Kentucky. They used to run the horses in the park, but the animals were tearing up the ground. Because of this, designated racetracks started popping up in Whitley County and neighboring towns.

He also had to chop wood daily to make sure there was enough wood stocked to survive the bitter winter months. KC helped on the farm every day with many of Peter's jobs. Liz sometimes put her hand in to help with the endless list of chores, but most of the time, she helped Mary in her garden and inside the home.

Once a week, Peter and Mary traveled into town with homemade household products, such as fabrics, candles, and soap, along with equipment for wagons and farming that Peter carved from wood. Like other families in Kentucky, they did not have much money. They often received needed products from bartering supplies. Each year, as the fall season came to an end, Peter took that time to inspect the chimney vent once more before the cold air arrived. It was something he did at least twice a year. This chore was necessary because the chimney would get clogged with too much soot and would result in cabin fever. This "cabin fever" was carbon monoxide poisoning that was caused by the door not being opened enough to bring in oxygen that was swallowed up by the fire and the family. Cabin fever was especially dangerous in the winter months. To clean the chimney, Peter dropped a live chicken down inside from the roof. The chicken would fight through the soot and come out at the bottom. It caused quite a mess for Mary to sweep up, but it managed to loosen the chunks of soot, rendering the chimney safe again. Either Mary or KC would catch the chicken as it came out in the fireplace. Whoever caught the chicken would quickly run him outside to be released in the chicken coop.

As Mary started preserving vegetables for the winter months, she was anxious to make a pot of Burgoo Stew. It was a favorite of hers and Peter's. Burgoo Stew was known as one of Kentucky's most famous dishes. Her mother passed on a recipe to her before she married Peter. His mother also passed on her version of the stew recipe. Most women on the prairie made the stew differently. Mary combined the two methods and made hers with turkey or chicken, mixed with red meat, tomatoes, lima beans, cabbage, corn, onions, carrots, and potatoes. She simmered the stew for 5-6 hours and as it cooked, she added peppers, curry powder, bourbon, spices, and herbs. The type and number of seasonings were up to the cook. She did not get to bake desserts often; that was a luxury.

Their favorite sweet treats were Apple Nut Cake and Blackberry Pie. She often made loaves of cornbread which they ate at breakfast and sometimes with their dinner. Peter also took cornbread with him when he was working on the farm. There was not much time to stop and eat. When he got hungry, he would take bites from the slices of cornbread that he kept in a folded napkin.

By November 1846, two years after they were married and three months before KC turned a year old, Mary was pregnant with her second child. As she did with KC, Mary worked until the day she went into labor. The last three months were the most difficult for her. There were no opportunities for her to take a break from her duties as wife and mother. The pregnancy was draining her energy. KC and the baby inside of her kept waking her up every few hours. But Mary mustered up the strength to carry on with her days. KC's baby clothes would be passed down to the new baby. Babies always shared clothes with their siblings, whether they were male or female. They shared pants, nightgowns, and even dresses. She continued to make clothes for KC since he appeared to be growing by the day. The bulk of her new baby's clothes would be hand-me-downs.

On August 12, 1847, Mary gave birth to Basheba "Liz" Harman. After Liz's birth, Mary rested for one day and was back to working in her garden and home. By the end of September, she had finished picking the vegetables from the garden. This work was not an easy task since there were a few hundred plants. Now was the time to transfer plants to the root cellar, clean the vegetables, and finish the process of preservation. August was the hottest month with temperatures often above 90 degrees. The heat never slowed her down.

~~~ Apple Nut Cake ~~~

Ingredients:
1 Cup Flour
1 tsp. Baking Soda
1 tsp. Ground Cinnamon
½ tsp. Salt
1 Cup Sugar
1 Egg
¼ Cup Vegetable Oil
2 Cups of Apples (peeled, cored, and chopped)
½ Cup Walnuts
½ Cup of Raisins or Dates

- Preheat oven to 350 degrees. Grease and flour an 8" loaf pan.
- Sift together the flour, baking soda, cinnamon, and salt. Set aside.
- In a medium bowl, mix the sugar, the egg, and the oil.
- Stir in the flour mixture until combined. Mix in the apples, nuts, and raisins.
- Bake for 55—60 minutes, or until a toothpick inserted in the middle comes out clean.

Chapter 5

K C was five years old when his dad started training him on the simple tasks of farming, such as mending fences, shearing sheep, milking cows, and caring for the animals. This would also be the first winter that KC followed his dad on hunting and fishing trips. Peter was going to teach him to trap animals, to know which vegetation was safe to eat, and how to spot snakes and other dangers by the tracks they left in the soil and grass. They took trips to the lake where KC learned to catch fish and frogs for meals. They hunted squirrels and deer for the meat. Bears were a popular animal to hunt and were treated in the same way as pigs, by giving the farmers bear hams and bear bacon.

They sold beaver and raccoon pelts to hat makers. They traded deerskin for a number of uses, including hats and gloves, and even bookbinding. With rabbit fur, they made shawls for trading and bartering at the general store.

Every evening, Mary gave KC and Liz lessons in math, reading, writing, and even in the Bible. She hoped to one day send them to school, but she wanted to teach them, just in case the chance did not arrive.

At four years old, Liz was helping her mother to clean, wash clothes, and to bake bread, butter, and pies. She was even learning to make soap. It was not difficult to make soap, but it took a while. First, they filled up a tub with ashes that they collected from the fireplace. After that, they poured rainwater on top. It soaked through the ashes and filtered through a hole at the bottom, where it filled the second bucket. This was called, "lye water." The lye water was then boiled with cooking grease and let to cool. The result as—soap! On Saturday, each member of the family took turns taking their weekly bath.

Shortly after Mary and Liz planted the last rows of seeds, she became pregnant with her third child. With each child, Mary worked until the day she went into labor. However, with this pregnancy, she felt different. She tired more easily during the day. It was more difficult to fall asleep at night. Even her morning sickness lasted several weeks longer than normal. Mary wondered if it was just from being pregnant three times. Maybe it was harder on her body than it was for others. Maybe her body was wearing out. Surviving childbirth was always a concern—and fear— for prairie women and Mary was no exception. She knew several women who died giving birth. So, when she went into labor two months early, it was pretty scary for her. And, of course, for Peter, too.

Peter was still working long hours during the day, and he regretted that he couldn't be there all the time for Mary during her difficult labor. He was almost finished harvesting the oats, sweet corn, and field corn. He sold the crop between September and May. He worked as quickly as he could so he could be home early for her.

Mary spent almost two days in labor. KC and Liz helped with household chores. Neighbors brought dinner and freshly baked loaves of Salt Rising Bread for Peter and the children. When Peter arrived home at night, the first thing he did was check on Mary. Then the two of them clasped their hands together and prayed for her and the baby. The midwife stayed by Mary's side until the time came for delivery. Mary gave birth to Ezra on Friday, December 12, 1851.

He was small and had difficulty breathing, but he appeared healthy. Mary's labor stopped, but her discomfort lingered. When the doctor stopped by later that day to examine Mary and the baby, he realized that she was still pregnant. Mary was having twins. One of the babies was born early. There was no way of knowing if the second baby was still alive. Though the labor pains stopped, the doctor told Mary to stay in bed. He was confident that the second baby would come at any time. He stayed by her side the rest of the night.

Mary stayed in bed for two more days. She assured the doctor that the labor had stopped, and she knew the second baby was still alive because he was back to kicking her in the ribs. She went back to her duties as wife and mother and waited for the day that Ezra's twin decided to join him. The midwife decided to stay at Peter's and Mary's home until the second baby was born. For the next couple of weeks, Mary awoke several times a night to shift Ezra in his bed to a new sleeping position. Mary and the doctor believed that this would help to shape his soft skull. He was kept near the window because the doctor said the cool draft was good for his tiny lungs.

During this time, Mary also continued to give KC and Liz their daily lessons. The midwife helped to prepare meals and wash the clothes. The frigid cold of the winter months would sometimes cause the well water to freeze. When that happened, the midwife and the children would carry in buckets of snow to melt over the fireplace. This gave them the water they needed to wash the clothes and even to make coffee.

Ezra's twin, Uhel Harman was born over two months later on Saturday, February 21, 1852. This time, Mary was in labor for one day. The doctor was sent for immediately, as he wanted to see for himself if the delivery of the second baby would be different in any way. There was not much known, at the time, on how or why this happened to women. Midwives knew more about pregnancy and childbirth than doctors. Doctors received most of their education on childbirth from experience. Since the boys were born two months apart, they were not noted publicly as twins.

Cleaning cloth diapers proved to be quite a chore for Mary. Liz also helped with diaper duty for Ezra and Uhel. First, the diapers had to be boiled and then hung on the line to dry. In the winter they would freeze. When they were taken down, they would bend the diapers over and over until they snapped, and the ice crystals broke off. Then they were to be hung up again on a clothesline in the house. Meantime, Uhel and Ezra were left bare. They could only hope that the boys would not go to the bathroom until the cloth diapers were clean. This was not always the case.

Though the entire family worked hard, there were occasions when the family had fun days together. On these occasions, they would have a picnic lunch by the river and would spend the day catching frogs, flying kites, and fishing.

The family had been attending Jellico Creek Baptist Church for the past four years. Every fall, the church had a community picnic that lasted all day. There were long tables set up adjacent to the church, and every family brought their share of food and tableware. The menu included bowls of delicious meat, loaves of bread, and vegetables. There were also rows of baked treats that were seldom enjoyed by children the rest of the year. There was a variety of pies baked by the women who were competing in the Pie Bake-Off. The highlight for the children was the red & white striped bags filled with candy. The general store always donated these.

After the meal, there were horse races and horseshoe pitching. The children also had their races and played games like Annie Over. To play Annie Over, the children broke off into two teams. They stood on opposite sides of a log. The team with the ball was It. One of the players would yell "Annie" and throw the ball to a child on the opposing team. If he or she caught the ball, then the teams would run to switch sides.

Meanwhile, the one who caught the ball would try to hit a player on the other team. If they hit an opposing player, then that child would join their team. In the end, the side with the most players won the game.

The country was just learning to play baseball. The love for the game was quickly absorbed by the children (and even most of the men) in town. No one was certain, at first, what the official rules of the games were. This often-caused disputes. When that happened, one of the parents would step up and answer any questions. And what they said was final.

Soon, for both boys and girls, it was game on!

The night ended with music and dancing.

On February 3, 1855, a brutal winter storm roared through the state of Kentucky. With it came bitter cold temperatures and veracious winds. By the end of the day, the Ohio River had frozen solid. KC and Liz were among a group of the children who took advantage of the icy river to sled on top and to slide on across on their boots. The river stayed frozen for 11 days.

When chunks of ice started to crack and break free, their fun came to an end.

On Monday, February 26, 1855, just twelve days after the storm released its grip on the community, the Harman family grew to include Curns Gillis Harman.

Jane Harman would follow two years later, on February 23, 1857. She was also born on a Monday. Within a year, the Harman family was about to grow once more. Mary was pregnant with her 7th child.

KC and Liz had been attending public school for the past five years.

Ezra and Uhel were both seven years old and just started attending classes with them. Liz was responsible for walking Uhel and Ezra to school and watching the younger children when she got home. She kept them entertained playing with dolls that Peter made out of rags and corn husks. She told them stories. They played guessing games and sang songs. Some of the songs they enjoyed were Minnie Myrtle, Have You Seen Sam, and Old Bob Ridley.

A few days before Mary went into labor, she became sick with muscle weakness, chills, and a fever. Pregnant women often picked up infections from working around the farm animals which could be what caused Mary's illness. Mary sent for her brother, Horatio Creekmore, to help her. He just returned from New York after graduating from medical school only a few months prior. The town was building a house for Horatio and his wife, Narcissa Farris; they called it "a log rolling."

To reach Mary's home, he had to cross the Cumberland River. Halfway across, his horse slipped and fell into the water. They both drowned. When Mary's son was born on Monday, June 6, 1859, she named him Horatio, after her brother. She even nicknamed him Doc. Mary became pregnant again when Doc was seven months old.

Sadly, terrible fate was about to befall the Harman family once more. In December, shortly before Christmas, Jane fell ill with pneumonia. Poor Jane suffered from coughing, chills, muscle aches, fever, and had difficulty breathing. Mary and Liz took turns staying by her bedside and used cold washcloths to bring down her temperature, along with alcohol rubs. They gave her a spoonful of Opium for her pain. Sadly, young Jane succumbed to the chokehold that pneumonia held over her tiny body. For the past two years, a number of children in Whitley County became sick with pneumonia. The epidemic seemed to be leaving the area but not until it claimed the life of Jane. She died on Monday, January 7, 1861. She was buried in an unmarked grave in Jellico Creek.

This was the first time that Peter and Mary had to bury a child. Mary was crushed. She knew she had to help the children through their grief and tried to stay strong for them. But there were days that she broke and could not hide her sadness. It was on these days that Liz stepped up and carried on the household duties for Mary. When Mary gave birth to Louraney "Lou"

Harman on Thursday, April 18, 1861, the soft cries of the new baby and her shining smile helped ease the family through their dark days. Peter suffered the loss of Jane in silence because men were told not to cry. At night while his children and wife slept, he sat in front of the fireplace, his face buried in his hands and wept silent tears.

~~~~ Salt Rising Bread ~~~~

Ingredients:
1 Cup Flour
1 tsp. Baking Soda
1 tsp. Ground Cinnamon
½ tsp. Salt
1 Cup Sugar
1 Egg
¼ Cup Vegetable Oil
2 Cups of Apples (peeled, cored, and chopped)
½ Cup Walnuts
½ Cup of Raisins or Dates

- Preheat Oven to 350 degrees. Grease and flour an 8" loaf pan.
- Sift together the flour, baking soda, cinnamon, and salt. Set aside.
- In a medium bowl, mix the sugar, the egg, and the oil.
- Stir in the flour mixture until combined. Mix in the apples, nuts, and raisins. Bake for 55—60 minutes, or until a toothpick inserted in the middle comes out clean

Chapter 6

Jellico Creek Schoolhouse
October 1861

KC reached across the bed to shake Ezra and Uhel to wake them for school. He turned to check on Curns who was already awake and sitting on the edge of the bed. They tiredly protested but did as he told them to do. He helped each one to get dressed and brushed their hair.

Liz dressed for the day. She pulled her hair back with a ribbon and grabbed Curns by the hand to help him down to the kitchen. Doc and Lou were fussing in the crib they shared. She gathered fresh cloth diapers to change them both. After she placed them in their highchairs, she and Curns went out to sweep the chicken coop and collect eggs.

KC was no longer in school, so before he sat down to breakfast, he gave water to the animals and cleaned the cow barn. When he was finished eating, he went to work on the farm and in the orchards with Peter. On occasion, they went hunting and fishing with Ezra and Uhel in tow. The boys did not attend school on those days.

At the start of Mary's daily routine, she toasted bread by the fireplace and cooked breakfast for the family. The fireplace had many uses. Mary also hung slices of metal over the fire for ironing clothes later. If she hung them up early in the morning, they would be ready by the afternoon. Once they were red hot, she placed them in the back compartment of her flat iron. Yes, she often burned the tips of her fingers. Several pieces of iron were hung at one time so that as one cooled, she could replace it with another.

There was usually baking to do so she carefully loaded wood into the oven next to the fireplace. It took two hours for the oven to be hot enough for baking.

Soon they were all at the breakfast table for a meal of porridge, eggs, sausage, and biscuits spread with raspberry preserves. Some mornings, they had bowls of popcorn cereal (popcorn mixed with milk and drizzled in honey). Mary fed herself last if there was food leftover.

Liz, Ezra, and Uhel each had a slate and a stick of chalk for schoolwork. Ezra and Uhel used a rag to clean their slate after the teacher inspected their work. However, there wasn't always one available. When that happened, they would spit on their slate and wipe it off with their sleeve. A paper tablet was expensive. So, they would only use it for penmanship classes. During those lessons they used a slate pencil or steel dipped pens that they dipped into inkwells. KC was guilty of once dipping a girl's braids into the ink.

They carried their lunches in metal pails that were once lard buckets. Lunch was either a piece of meat and a biscuit or a chunk of bread topped with either bacon grease or preserves. Sometimes their lunch included an apple, hard-boiled eggs, a sweet potato, or a slice of apple or berry dumpling. In the winter, the Harman kids, along with several others in the class, would bring a potato from the garden. Their teacher would put them all in an iron bucket and hang it by the heater, by lunchtime they had hot baked potatoes. Each one of them would scratch their initials in their potato so they could tell them apart later.

The journey to school was as difficult as the classes themselves. Schools were spaced 5 miles apart because they thought it was close enough to walk. There were never any school delays or cancellations for inclement weather.

As Ezra and Uhel got older, their chores extended outside the home to the school. They took turns with other students to haul buckets of water from a nearby farm to the one-room schoolhouse. This was the job of the boys in seventh and eighth grade. Once there, they would take turns filling the school pitcher with water. There was a single tin cup that the students shared during the day. After lunch, the cup would be passed around once more so everyone one could get a cup of water to drink.

During the school year, Peter and Mary cut back on the kid's chores at home. The school year was 132 days long and included a summer term and winter term. Each term was approximately ten weeks. The children did not attend school during the spring and fall because they were needed at home to help with the harvest. There was a pot-bellied stove in the middle of the classroom that would heat the school in the winter. During those months, the older students would take turns hauling wood daily to keep the fire going. Sometimes they had to walk a distance of 100 yards with their bundle of firewood.

Classes started at 9 AM and were over by 2:00. At the start of each day, the teacher stood at the door and rang the handbell until the last student entered. The boys and girls entered through separate sides of the doorway and sat on opposite sides of the room. The school desks were not exactly made for comfort. The seats were handmade and could fit up to 4 children.

Curns was pretty excited for this day to begin because this was his first day at school. He would be in the Abecedarians, (that is pronounced: ay-bee-see- dair-uns). He and his classmates sat in the front row. The main focus of their group was to learn their ABC's. Liz sat in the back of the room with the older children. They were given time to read lessons in their textbooks each day. Then random students would be called upon to go to the front of the classroom to "hear their lesson." After that, each grade went to the front of the room for daily recitations. The older students were used to help teach the younger students. Liz was often paired off with younger children who were struggling. She would spend the day tutoring them. She and the other girls always enjoyed these days.

There was no standard set of books. At times, the school received a variety of books to pass out to students in need. Children could also use books that their parents were able to purchase or books they borrowed from cousins or siblings. Liz had the McGuffey's Spelling Book that was passed down to her from KC. Ezra and Uhel used Appleton's School Reader.

Curns used the ABC Hornbook in America. Not all the children could afford books. Uhel and Ezra's books were passed down from KC and Liz. The younger students in the class learned the bulk of their work by listening to the others recite what they just read.

For a small country school, there was a wealth of information to be absorbed. The Harman children soaked in all of the knowledge that was available, including reading, American history, math, spelling, grammar, geography, arithmetic, writing, and English. They also had lessons on manners and rhetoric (communication).

The year prior, in November 1860, the country held their 16th Presidential election—the winner was Abraham Lincoln. Their teacher turned the election into a lesson on American politics. Lincoln ran against—and defeated—Southern Democrat John Breckinridge, Union Candidate John Bell, and US Senator Stephen Douglas. One of the reasons this election was so monumental was that Lincoln was the first member of the newly formed Republican party to be elected President of the United States. Douglas was his chief competitor in the election. The stance most important during the debates was the issue of slavery. The Democrats were strong supporters of slavery and Lincoln wanted it banished across the country.

The Harman children were mindful of obeying their teacher. Discipline included getting cracked on their knuckles or their palms with a ruler, being forced to hold a heavy book for an hour, or writing, "I will not" do a specific activity 100 times on the blackboard. Sometimes one of the boys would be punished by having to wear a girl's bonnet and made to sit on the girl's side of the classroom. If their teacher saw it fit, the student would also get a lashing.

The only rule to that was the children would not be hit on the head. The Board of Education decided the disruptive behavior and the number of lashings.

There was a strict rule of NO TALKING unless the teacher called upon them. They were not even allowed to whisper. If they had questions, they raised their hand to ask for permission to speak.

Recess was called nooning. It was an hour long and started at 11:00. The teacher was pretty lenient on the rules when it came time to recess. This was a chance for the kids to relieve stress and run off some steam, so most activities were allowed. During recess, they sang songs, such as De' Old Grey Goose, Over the River, Yankee Doodle, The Day Star of Freedom, To the Boy Defender of Kentucky's Honor, and Blue-Eyed Jane. Some of them brought toys from their homes, such as jacks, marbles, dolls, and leather balls. They also played games like Tag, Hide-and-Seek, Duck on the Rock, Run Sheep Run, and Prisoner's Base. The rules of the games were simple.

Duck on the Rock: A large stone (called the duck) is placed on a larger stone or log. As one player stands near the rock, to guard it, other students throw rocks to try and knock it off.

Run Sheep Run: The students split into two teams—the sheep and the foxes. The "sheep" picked one player on their side to be the "old ram."

63

He/she is the one who decides where all the sheep will hide. They all hide together. His part in the game is to lead them back to the goal. The side of the foxes searches for the sheep, also as a team. As they search, the "old ram" stays by them and shouts out commands in a code to the sheep in hiding. The commands are decided on at the start of the game. Some examples include:

"Red" means "Danger."

"Green" means "Go around to the left."

"Blue" means "Go around to the right."

"Purple" means "Stand still."

"Yellow" means "Keep on going in the same direction and get closer to the goal."

When he thinks the coast is clear, or if one of the foxes have spotted his team, he shouts, "Run Sheep Run!" All the sheep and foxes then run for the goal. The player who reaches the goal first wins the game for his team. If the sheep win, they get to be the foxes in the next game.

Prisoner's Base: The class was divided into two teams. There was a line of chalk drawn between them. About 20 feet behind each team, they drew a square. On each side, a player from the opposite team stood in the square, or what they called "the prison." One of their teammates would try to reach the "prison" without being caught. If they made it, then the two of them would try to run back without being caught. If they were caught, then they would both become "prisoners." Both sides would try to escape at the same time. At the end of recess, the team with the most prisoners won the game.

Liz was fortunate to gain the education that she had. Most girls didn't learn to read and write because families did not think it was important for girls to receive an education. They were said to be "innocent of book learning." She was now in eighth grade. If she did not have to leave school, she would graduate after the spring session. She often had left school year early to help Mary as KC often had to do for Peter.

To graduate, Liz would have to pass the final exam. It would take 5 hours to complete. She would have an hour for grammar, 45 minutes for US history, 1 Hour for orthography and 1 hour for geography. She would also get an hour break for lunch. Some of the questions on the test would include the following:

1. District No. 33 has a valuation of $35,000. What is the necessary levy to carry on a school seven months at $50 per month, and have $104 for incidentals?"
2. Write in words the following:
   5764; .000003;123416; 653.0965; 43.37
3. Solve: 35-7 plus 4, 5-8 plus 5-14-59.112
4. Find the costs at 12 ½ cents per square yard of kalsomining the walls of a room 20 feet long, 16 feet wide, and 9 feet high, deducting 1 door 8 ft. by 4 ft. 6 in. and two windows 5 ft. by 3 ft. 6 in. each. *(By the way, kalsomining is a low-cost type of paint made from lime)*.
5. A man bought a farm for $2400 and sold it for $2700. What percent did he gain?
6. A man sold a watch for $180 and lost 16 2/3%. What was the original cost of the watch?
7. Find the amount of $50.30 for 3 years, 3 months, and 3 days, at percent.
8. Name the parts of speech and define those that have no modification.
9. A wagon box is 2 feet deep, 10 feet long, and 3 feet wide. How many bushels of wheat will it hold?
10. What are elementary sounds and how are they classified?

Once Liz was graduated from school, her workload at home would increase to include cooking, milking the cows and goats, spinning and weaving wool from the sheep, sewing clothes/blankets, preserving food, churning butter, making bread, cleaning the house, washing clothes, and making candles to barter with at the general store.

Their teacher was paid $22 a month (female teachers earned $8-$12 a month). Every five years, he was offered a raise of 25 cents per week as long as the Board of Education approved it. He was required to "lay aside from each pay a goodly sum of his earnings for his benefit during his declining years so that he will not become a burden on society." To earn his Teaching Certificate, he had to attend classes that cost $37.50. These are

some of the classes he had to take:
- Mental Arithmetic
- Written Arithmetic
- Reading
- Penmanship
- US History
- Civil Government
- Geography
- English Grammar
- English Composition
- Drawing Blackboard
- Bookkeeping
- Physiology
- Theory and Art of Teaching
- Orthography (spelling, hyphenation, capitalization, word breaks, and punctuation)

There were also classes on hygiene, recreational activity, curricular problems, and classroom teaching.

Male teachers were titled schoolmaster, and the female teachers were titled either a schoolmarm or schoolmistress. All of the teachers followed a strict code of conduct. Those rules included the following: filling the lamps and cleaning the chimney every morning. At the start of each day, he also whittled pencils to sharpen them for the students.

Since the Harman's teacher was a man, he was allowed to take one night a week for courting. He was given two nights if he attended church regularly. His fellow female teachers were not allowed to court, nor were they allowed to marry.

He could also be fired if he was seen smoking, using liquor in any form, frequenting pool or public halls, or getting shaved in a barbershop. They thought that such actions showed a lack of morals.

~~~~ **Blue Eyed Jane** ~~~~
Jimmie Rodgers

The sweetest girl in the world
Is my blue eyed Jane
We fell in love like turtledoves
While the moon was shining down
I asked her then,
I asked her when
Wedding bells would ring
She said "Oh, dear, it seems so queer
That this could happen here."

You are my little pal
And I never knew a sweeter gal
My little, blue-eyed Jane
I love you so
And when the sun goes down
And the shadow's creeping over town
Just meet me in the lane
My blue-eyed Jane

Jane dear, listen here
I've come to say farewell
The world is drear without you, dear
But now I cannot linger here
I'm going away this very day
Oh please, come go with me
I'll be sad and blue wanting you

Longing all day through.
My little blue-eyed Jane
You'll always be the same sweet thing
I know you'll never change

I love you so
And when the sun goes down
And the shadow's creeping over town
Then I'll come back again
My blue-eyed Jane And when the sun goes down
And the shadow's creeping over town
Then I'll come back again
My blue-eyed Jane

Chapter 7

The Harman Farms
April 1868

Before the sun began to peer in the morning sky, Peter and Mary were already awake and prepared to start their day. Still sleepy, Peter got dressed in the dim light of the lantern that rested on his dresser. He walked to the washing-stand and cupping his hands, he rubbed his eyes to help gather his second wind. As he poured the warm water from the pitcher, he heard Mary rustling in the kitchen.

It was the job of the boys in the family to carry in arms full of firewood and buckets of water for their mother. In the winter months, they also had to fill their father's water pitcher for the washing stand with warm water from the fireplace. It was generally filled the night before but, in the winter, the cold nights would freeze the water.

The Harman family flourished over the previous years. Mary and Peter welcomed their tenth baby, Peter Frank Harman, on Monday, April 30, 1866. A string of exciting changes was about to stir things up in the family, and Peter's birth was just the beginning.

It was only 22 years earlier that Peter and Mary wed, and now they were standing arm-in-arm as they watched their daughter, Liz, walk down the aisle to marry Joe Ryan. He was a quiet young man, and most of his past was somewhat of a mystery. Nonetheless, he was a hard-working farmer who loved Liz and was welcomed by the Harman family.

Several months later, on Thursday, January 3, 1867, KC married Elender (Ellen) Smith. Their marriage would grow to be as solid and true as Mary's and Peter's. Their first child, Ed Harman, was born nine months later on Saturday, October 12, 1867. Three months after Ed was born, Liz gave birth to her first baby, a boy she named Joe Ryan, Jr. He was born on Friday, January 10, 1868. One wedding after another means plenty of wedding cake, not to mention heart-warming soups, and side dishes, such as squash pudding, beef olives, and corn fritters.

Life for Peter and Mary was pretty overwhelming at that point. They had just welcomed their first two grandchildren into the world. They had eight children at home, particularly a one-year-old boy, and Mary was pregnant with a little girl. Her baby was born five days before Liz's son.

Overwhelming—Yes! But never disappointing, for in the Harman family, it only meant more people to love, cherish, and protect. Though Ellen was a new bride and a new mother, she still did everything that she could to help her new sister-in-law, Liz, and Mary with their babies. She was so appreciative that Mary graced her new daughter with Ellen's name. And so, on Sunday, January 5, 1868, Jaley Ellen Harman was born.

Though labor and delivery were always difficult for women, doctors continued to find ways to ease their pain. Using chloroform during delivery was becoming more common. This was done by soaking a rag in chloroform and having the mother hold it up to her face and breathe it in; sometimes it put her to sleep. The danger to that was that it could also put the baby to sleep, and he could suffocate during delivery. There was clergy who spoke out against any form of assistance claiming that labor pain was God's will.

Additions added to the home to accommodate the new family members included a parlor, a separate washroom, and several bedrooms. Their beds were also made by Peter, from a thick cloth stuffed with straw. The mattress was laid on top of a set of ropes that were tied together in tight rows. This is what they used as their "box springs."

They added a pantry to the kitchen. A pitcher pump was built alongside the home to limit trips to the creek for buckets of water. A large cistern was also added to collect rainwater.

There was a 2-hole outdoor privy about 100 feet from the house.

Though dry weather forced most families either further west or to back trail east, the Harman's were standing firm to their ground. The laborious work of a farmer could not be relieved by moving to fresh ground. Peter knew this, and for the sake of his family, he pushed through the long hours, unpredictable elements, and the uncertainty of it all, with just his faith and love for his family to carry him through. He and other farmers of Whitley County were still recovering from the wrath of the Civil War that was left behind by soldiers. Peter and his neighbors often found themselves at the mercy of both Union and Confederate soldiers. Both Union and Confederate soldiers invaded their homes and stole food from their crops. The soldiers were allowed to take, at will, what they wanted if they claimed they needed it to fight the war. Kentucky was not considered a part of the Midwest and was one state away from the east coast territory. So, they branded themselves a 'southeastern state' and remained neutral during the war. Ironically, Kentucky was the birthplace of Abraham Lincoln and Confederate President Jefferson Davis. They were both born in log cabins, one year apart, and lived 100 miles from each other.

Through the years, Peter expanded his farm, allowing him to feed and support his growing family needs. His now, 40' x 60' barn included an addition on one end used for storage. There was a three-stall wagon shed and a cow barn that provided space for hay storage in the loft with room below for 12-cow stanchions. A silo and a corn crib stood adjacent to the barn. Inclement weather was the farmer's biggest enemy. On some days, the wind blew like thunder and made work more difficult. Too much rain could create numerous problems for Peter. The biggest of them all was flooding. April, May and June were the months when it rained the most. They had to keep an eye on the barns, as well as the farm. If the water started to fill the barn, they had to dig a ditch through the stable to keep the water drained from around the horses.

But Peter had even more worries than that. If the crops sat too long in standing water, the stems of the plant would start to rot, and the leaves began to yellow. He also was not able to get the wagons out in the thick mud. If Peter walked through the mud or tried to drag farm equipment through it, it would compress the mud, limiting crop growth. He was not able to plant new crops because the mud blocked the air from reaching the seeds and it made it harder for the plants to pop out of the ground. There were times when Peter and his sons needed to expand the farm, but the ground was so wet that they struggled to remove trees and stumps to make room for new crops.

The increase in the rain also meant an increase in bugs. If Peter could not get out to the fields, he would not be able to get the problem of bugs under control in time, which put his crops at further risk. Then there were the weeds. They grew quickly and everywhere after a long rain.

Snow was beneficial during the winter months. However, that too could quickly become problematic to Peter's crops if that snow included hail. It had happened to him once already. It was devastating for Peter. After all of the long hours working under the heat of the blazing sun, day after day, his crops were destroyed after only 2 hours of a crippling hailstorm. If a great deal of ice followed the snow, then it could destroy the crops. Too much snow could also cause the roofs of the barn to collapse. When the snow melted in the spring, it was refreshing for the soil. If there was too much snow, then there was a risk of flooding. Peter acquired a new Hereford cow and one day, after KC had returned the older cows to their stalls, the Hereford bolted from the yard. KC was in hot pursuit as the cow trotted across the farm down the road onto a neighbor's farm and headed straight for town. A local farmer spotted the chase and assisted KC in capturing the cow and returning it home. Peter later told KC that he should have ignored the cow because it would have grazed nearby and rejoined the herd later that day.

There was now a spring house with water piped to a watering trough for the horses. The horse stable, chicken coop, and pigpen were all enlarged. More animals also meant more risks for Peter and the children. The bulls could gore them, and the pigs could bite them. They could get pecked by the chickens, kicked by horses when they were treating thrush on their hooves with iodine. They could also get kicked when they were trimming the hooves of the horses. The roosters tried to bite them when they were clipping their spurs, as well as the dogs, that nipped at them when they had to trim their claws. Peter showed them how to sew their cuts and treat them with alcohol that Mary made.

They added tamed rabbits and sheep to the farm. Their wool from the sheep was used to make clothes. The sheep were sheered every spring, using hand shears that were kept sharp. Every two fleeces were rolled and tied together and put in 100-pound feed bags. When it came time to get new clothes, Mary and Peter made most of what they needed, rarely buying clothes from stores. This was a herculean task, and all family members participated. Some of Peter's and Mary's sisters and brothers chipped in on the work. Their first job was to shear the sheep. Afterward, Mary and the rest of the women washed the wool 2–3 times. When they thought they cleaned it thoroughly enough, it was then left out in the sun to dry. Once it was dry, the ladies picked through the fleece, pulling out seeds, sticks and pebbles picked up by the sheep in the fields. This was a painstaking chore. The wool was then carded and carried over to the spinning wheel.

Carding is basically combing the fiber (wool, flax, etc.), making it lie flat and in one direction, and also to remove unwanted particulate. It would be rolled off the cards (flat or gently rounded boars with nails or metal tines) and into large rolls that would then become roving. The roving would be spun on the wheel into different-sized thread or yarn depending on the end purpose, whether it be socks, underwear, clothes, rugs, etc.

The finished material was then dyed over a cooking fire. Colors were created by using flower petals, plants, and berries. Since making clothes was such a long and challenging process, clothes were continuously remade until they ended up in the rag bag.

The wool that was not used by the family was shipped by railroad to the buyers. It would take up to 10 days for businesses to pick up the wool, and for a check to be released to Peter. It then took 8-10 days for a check to arrive.

Laundry day was a long day for Mary, Ellen, and Liz. Even 12-year-old Lou and 10-year-old Mary helped out. They washed the clothes by the creek in the summer. During the colder months, they boiled water over a fire in the backyard. There was a separate pot for rinse water. They shaved a whole cake of soap into the pot of water over the fire.

While preparing the water, they sorted the clothes into three piles—one pile was whites, another was colored clothes, and the third pile was work clothes and rags. They made their starch for the colored clothes by mixing flour and cool water and thinning it down with boiling water. The dirty spots on the clothes were scrubbed over the washboard before they added them to the water. Once added to the water, they were stirred and removed with the use of a broom handle. Once the clothes were washed, rinsed, and wrung out, they were hung out on a clothesline to dry. They laid the towels in the grass and hung the rags over the fence. After that, they poured the rinse water in the garden or the flower bed and used the hot soapy water to scrub the porch.

In 1869, the school year was extended to 180 days. Classes now ran from September to May. The rule was mandatory across the country. That meant most of the Harman children would not be graduating. They were needed on the farm and to help Mary in the home. There were plenty of chores to go around, such as cleaning the barns, spreading manure, repairing horse-powered equipment and vehicles, mending tack, and feeding the animals (morning and evening). Feeding the horses meant grain and hay had to be planted, tended, harvested, shocked, threshed, baled, hauled, and stacked.

Ezra and Uhel used to turn some of the chores into a competition like who could shear the most sheep and who was a better pitcher in the hay barn. They had a way of turning all of their chores into a race. Who could shuck corn the fastest? Who could gather the most berries? Who could card wool the fastest? Curns and Doc often joined in their competitions.

~~~~ Squash Pudding ~~~~

Ingredients:
Salt
Nutmeg
Sugar
1 Squash
6 Large Apples
1 Pint Milk or Cream
3-4 Slices Dried Bread
2 Tbsp. Rose Water
2 Tbsp. Wine
1 Tbsp. Flour
5-6 eggs

- Preheat Oven to 400 degrees.
- Core, boil, and skin the squash.
- With each apple-pare, core, and stew until tender.
- Mix the apples and squash together.
- Squash the dry bread into a powder (or use unseasoned breadcrumbs). Add 6-7 spoonsful to the squash/apple mixture.
- Add milk/cream, rose water, and wine.
- Beat the eggs, strain them and add to the mixture.
- In a separate bowl combine salt, nutmeg, and sugar until it reaches your desired taste. Add to the mixture.
- Add flour. Beat together. Bake for 40-50 minutes.

Chapter 8

---◆●●◆---

Holidays on the Farm
February 1873

I t's true that Peter and Mary worked tirelessly from morning till night but make no mistake, they had their fun days, too. The Harman children also found ways to have fun together. Tiddlywinks was one way they had fun, a game they could play with their friends, too. Players used a large disc, called a shooter, to flip smaller discs, called winks, into a cup. The player to get all of his winks into the cup first, wins the game. They often spent time alone to practice flipping winks.

Along with trains, marbles, jump ropes, and ball games, they played dominoes, made from ivory. The key rule with shooting marbles is that one knuckle had to be on the ground when the player flicked the "shooter" marble. Jackstraws was also a favorite game of theirs. It later became known as Pick-Up Sticks. When the Harman's played, they used straw or sticks that, like the dominoes, were made from ivory.

Snakes and Ladders, later known as Chutes and Ladders, was a game used to teach morals. As you see, each time the player slid back, it was after he did something naughty. Instead of dice, they used a teetotum, which was a spinning top with numbers written on it. When it stopped spinning and fell on its side, the number facing up was the number of moves each player would take. Dice were taboo for children because adults associated them with gambling.

Toys were not always available. At those times, the Harman's and their friends put their imaginations to work. Along with hide-and-seek and tag, even shadow tag was a fun game to play. They could play with each other or with their friends at recess. The object of this game was to choose someone who was "it." They had to capture someone by stepping on their shadow. And that person would then be "it." And don't try cheating by hiding in the shadow of a tree or a barn because you would have by the count of ten to come out or automatically be "it."

The Hot and Cold Game could be played anywhere since it was played by hiding an object and the person searching for the object would be given clues as to where it was simply by shouting hot (if he was near it) and cold (as he got farther away). They were given a set amount of time to find it. That was usually a few minutes. There was a similar game played between two people. It started with one player hiding an object while the other closed their eyes and counted to 10. They would then uncover their eyes and begin the search, but this time there were no clues. The person who hid the object would count to 60, for that was all the time they had to find it.

A favorite day for the kids in town to play together, outside of school, was Sunday. It was considered a day of rest. After the Harman's attended church, they arrived home for a large meal and to greet visitors. Sunday was a day of rest—to attend church, visit friends, and receive callers. Sounds like fun, right? Well, it was not always fun for Mary, since it was her job to prepare this meal. The children chipped in, but it was Mary who did the brunt of the work because she wanted her family to enjoy their day of rest. She was indeed a selfless woman.

However, before church, there were still chores to do. The animals were fed and watered, and they had to milk the cows. They also cleaned the stables and added fresh bedding for the animals. After all, the animals were still in need of care. After that, the fun for the children began, which usually started with pony rides in the front yard with their friends.

Easter

With as steeped in Christianity as Peter and Mary were, Easter was a particularly important holiday. The family never missed a church service for Good Friday or Easter Sunday though they also followed the fun side of Easter for children. Every year in the days leading up to Easter, the children put together an Easter Tree. The tree was made of several tree branches gathered together and displayed in either a pot or a large basket. They donned the tree branches with decorated eggs that were hollowed out alongside several glass eggs. The day before Easter, the whole family painted Easter eggs. They took their favorite egg to church with them and participated in the Egg Roll. At home, they told stories about the resurrection of Christ and how important it was to remember that day. Before they went to bed, Peter entertained them with more stories about the Easter Bunny.

When they awoke the next morning, they found an Easter basket for each one of them that was left behind from Peter Cottontail. Inside the basket were a variety of nuts, fruit, and candy (not a large amount though). The types of candy included rock candy, a few Necco wafers, caramels (homemade by Mary), lemon drops, taffy, licorice sticks, and a single gumball, peppermint stick, gumdrop, a root beer barrel, and of course, a candy rabbit made from pastry and sugar. Soon the children were off to search for the painted Easter eggs that were now hidden outside the house (and even in the garden).

Then it was time for Easter dinner, sometimes relatives and neighbors dropped by to visit, so there was always extra food prepared. The savory Easter dinner included a glazed ham, roasted lamb, potato hash, deviled eggs, applesauce, corn, green beans, pickled eggs, and sweet potatoes. There were also hot cross buns, sprinkled with a sugary cross, and German Sweet Bread, nicknamed Niz. For dessert, there were strawberry shortcake and blueberry muffins.

May Day

They celebrated May Day with citywide community picnics and Maypole Dances. Since then, the rich meaning of the holiday had told a deeper more sinister side of America. In 1884, the Federation of Organized Trades and Labor Unions held a convention in Chicago, where they announced that the working American would no longer be forced into long days of hard labor by big businesses and that 8 hours was long enough. They stated that on May 1, 1886, workers everywhere would walk out to demonstrate their dedication to this cause. Most of the businesses dismissed their demand and did not take them seriously, claiming their workers would never participate in such an event.

The following year they, once again, announced their planned protest to take place on May 1, 1886. Days before the scheduled walk-out, newspapers urged Americans to participate in the protest to fight back against big businesses that used and abused them. They printed such statements as:

Workingmen to Arms!

One pound of DYNAMITE is worth more than a bushel of BALLOTS.

Sure enough, on May 1, 1886, more than 300,000 American workers from 13,000 businesses walked off their jobs in honor of the first May Day celebration. May Day is a day to honor the men who fought and died for the 8-hour workday: for the children who protested their treatment inside the industry walls and were beat down for it and for the people whose homes were burned to the ground (many people were inside those homes at the time). May America never forget the names of the men who made labor laws mandatory in America. May their names never be forgotten or wiped from the pages of history:

- Albert Parsons
- August Spies
- Louis Lingg
- Samuel Fielden
- Oscar Neebe
- Michael Schwabb
- George Engel
- Adolph Fischer

Independence Day

Independence Day was celebrated by all Americans as a day to honor the country's independence, democracy and freedoms. The celebrations started early in the morning with the sounds of bells ringing and rifles fired into the air. These were familiar sounds that filled the air as the day went on. For the Centennial celebration in 1876, the country celebrated for three days—from July 3rd to July 5th.

There was a community picnic that many people traveled miles to attend. Even the Harman's traveled 5 miles to participate in the day's events. Games at the picnic included races, watermelon eating contests, and baseball games. There was also fiddle music and plenty of dancing. The Fourth of July picnic included mouthwatering foods, such as hot dogs, crispy fried chicken, hot & spicy barbecue ribs, corn-on-the-cob, homemade pickles, potato salad, and of course, thick slices of sweet watermelon. For dessert, they had a choice of apple pie, peach cobbler, or cherry pie. The meal was topped off with tall glasses of lemonade or punch. In 1883 they added mugs of Dr. Pepper and Root Beer to the picnic.

At nightfall, there was a display of brightly colored fireworks that crackled and popped in the night sky. When Peter and Mary arrived home, they lit candles and displayed them by the windows.

In 1881, the government ordered a ban on all fireworks out of respect to the shooting of President Garfield. The incident happened on Saturday, July 2nd, shortly after 9:30 AM. He was just about to board a train at the Baltimore & Potomac Railroad Station in Washington DC, when Charles Guiteau shot him. They held prayer meetings for President Garfield instead of community picnics. President Garfield lived for several months after the shooting. He died on the morning of September 19th from infections that he received from doctors tending to his bullet wounds with unclean hands.

Halloween

Halloween was a spooky fun day for Mary's and Peter's children. A week before, they carved jack-o-lanterns and toasted pumpkin seeds over the fire. Every year, Peter would tell them the legendary story of the Jack-o-Lantern. As the story goes, there was a farmer named Jack who often played tricks on the Devil. His trickery resulted in him being turned away from both Heaven and Hell after he died. He made himself a lamp from a pumpkin and burned a lump of coal inside it. This kept the spirits away because when they saw it, they knew it was just Jack and his lantern. From that day onward, on Halloween, when the ghosts would walk the Earth, people would place Jack-O-Lanterns outside their homes to scare away the spirits.

When it came time to go trick-or-treating, Mary made costumes for the younger children with help from Liz. They dressed up as scarecrows, ghosts, clowns, Indians, monsters, and generally scary masks made from potato sacks or paper mache. They were not allowed to dress as witches or devils. Those costumes went against Mary's religious beliefs.

They traveled door-to-door gathering sweets, fruits, and other baked treats. Mary, herself, participated in the holiday, passing out cookies to children who stopped by the Harman home. Businesses in town stayed open to pass out candy and cups of apple cider. At the general store, they could stop and play a game of bobbing for apples.

Thanksgiving

Thanksgiving was declared a national holiday in 1863 by President Lincoln in an effort to mend forgiveness between the north and the south. On the Harman farm, this was indeed the most wholesome day of the year. Thanksgiving was a day for family to gather together leaving any potential ill-feelings at the door. This was the day to be appreciative of everything that they had. There were no regrets or disappointments for the things they could not afford. It was nothing but a day of Thanks. The signature dish of the day was turkey and giblet gravy. It was served with fish, rolls with melted butter, stuffing, olives, celery, oyster stew, fried smelts (small fish), creamed asparagus, dumplings, mashed potatoes, fried onions, cranberry sauce, and baked squash. To snack on, there were ample trays of vegetables, cheese, and mixed nuts. The dessert table was filled with custard, fruit pie, hickory nut cake (served with lemon jelly), almond ice cream, pumpkin pie, sweet potato pie, pecan pie, and ginger cake. Drinks served that day included hot chocolate and apple cider for the children. There was coffee, buttered rum, and eggnog for the adults.

Christmas

Christmas was a cherished American holiday, and the Harman's were no exception to that. Mary and Liz started to prepare the food for the Christmas dinner weeks in advance. Even the plum pudding was made days before Christmas. It was left to age in the pot until Christmas day. As the days etched closer to Christmas Eve, there were men with carts set up in town to sell ornaments, decorations, and Christmas cards. Peter always remembered to pick up a card for Mary. She told him that it was not necessary, but he knew that she deserved this small token to thank her for all that she did for her family throughout the year.

Peter and Mary were fighting horrendous snowstorms and bitter temperatures, but they always made sure that Christmas was still a special day, especially when it came time to decorate. Garland, made from pine, framed the doorways and window frames. The family decorated the tree with strings of popcorn, a paper chain, ribbons, gold stars, a variety of ornaments and angels, and a handmade tin star for the top of the tree.

The whole family counted down the days till Christmas Eve. On that night, they went to church service and then home to sing songs and tell stories about Santa Claus, who was on his way to the Harman house. Each one of them hung their Christmas stocking and was off to bed.

In the morning they rushed to the living room with excitement to see if Santa Claus had been there. Sure enough, there would be a pile of gifts in colored paper—one for each of the Harman children. Throughout the years, their gifts included rifles (for the boys), a terracotta ring for Liz, necklaces for the girls, a knitted scarf, drum and horn, handmade dolls, sleds, horses (carved from wood), marbles, and books. In each stocking, they had a piece of fruit, a piece of candy or a peppermint stick, a cookie or a small cake, and a shiny new penny. Peter would gift Mary with either a figurine, a bottle of perfume, or lace doilies. She often made him a new dress shirt for Sundays or mittens and a hat.

For breakfast, they had muffins, eggs, and mushrooms served on toast. And soon, relatives arrived for Christmas dinner which was a glorious feast. The main dish was roasted turkey or pheasant (depending on what KC and Peter were able to catch) and boiled ham. Along with those dishes, there were assorted vegetables, including potatoes and gravy, mashed turnips, corn, peas, carrots, and cauliflower cooked in butter. There was also cranberry sauce, applesauce, pickled beets, plum preserves on graham bread, salt rising bread, and cheese & crackers. Dinner was topped off with strong black coffee with cream and sugar.

There was a wide selection of sweet desserts for after dinner that was a rare treat for the family. These included fudge, fruit cake, mince pies, apple pie, cherry pie, and even a peach pie, along with the plum pudding, Yorkshire pudding, and Neapolitan cake. There was also a selection of cookies, such as macaroons, gingerbread men, honey cookies, sour cream cookies, and star-shaped sugar cookies.

During the Christmas season of 1889, President Benjamin Harrison had a beautiful Christmas tree proudly displayed in the window of the White House. When they decorated the tree, they used strands of gold tinsel, shiny glass balls, and figures of animals and holiday designs. This was the start of a yearly Christmas tradition for each President to share with the public.

Weeks later, on January 1st, President Harrison would also partake in a New Year's Day tradition where he stood on the front lawn and shook hands with hundreds of people lined up to shake his hand. Though it lasted several hours, he shook hands with each person, one by one and wished him a "Happy New Year."

At the Harman house, their New Year's Eve holiday started with a meal of pork, cabbage, and black-eyed peas. Mary also believed in serving circle shaped foods for her family—for luck. Some circle-shaped foods that she prepared were cake, cookies, oranges, biscuits, and apple fritters. At midnight, they toasted with glasses of grape juice and they each made a New Year's resolution. They ended the night singing songs and reflecting on all of the events of the previous year—the good and the bad—the picnics and playing games with their cousins and friends—and the long hours on the farm to the tireless days of gardening and making clothes. This was what made New Year's Eve special, looking around and realizing how far they had come. Mary and Peter swelled with pride. No matter what obstacles life threw at their feet, they marched on. They were happy to overcome life's challenges. They did all of it for their children. They did it to keep their family close and ever moving forward. They did it for the generations of Harman's who would follow in their footsteps. They did it because their family was everything to them.

~~~~ Yorkshire Pudding ~~~~

Ingredients:
Pan Drippings (from a meat dish)
1 Cup Milk
1 Cup Flour
2 Eggs
¼ tsp Salt

- Preheat oven to 450 degrees.
- Put drippings from meat dish in a pan.
- In a separate bowl, mix eggs, milk, flour, and salt. Pour into the pan with the drippings.

Bake for 30 minutes. The pudding is done when it is puffy and golden brown. Cut into squares.

A tintype of Mary Creekmore

Peter Harman (1823-1879)

Children of Peter and Mary Creekmore Harman Front Row (from left): Lou, Peter Frank, and Matt. Back Row (from left): KC, Uhel, Curns Sr., and Doc.

Peter Harman died in a stagecoach the day he and Mary arrived at their destination in Rock, Kansas 1879, Mary was buried in Verden, Okla. 1909.

Peter, Mary, and their children, all attended Jellico Creek Baptist Church.

An exceptional photo of KC and Ellen Harman

An early image of Babe and Nellie's home.
Seated in the picture are Babe Harmon, Nellie Harmon, Kenneth Swinney,
Idonia Harmon, Mrs. JW Gann, and Amy Ruth Gann.

Babe Harmon World War 1

Curns Harmon Sr.
From Whitley County, Kentucky to McClain County, Oklahoma.

An early military picture of Babe Harmon.

A photo of Curns Gillis Harmon Jr. taken in October 1931.
He was 22 years old.

Sad Papaw's grandmother, Nellie Harmon.
She is standing next to Mabel Harmon and her son, Wayne. Mabel was married to Buzz Harmon. They owned the Dibble Crossroad Store in the background. Buzz's grandson, Terry Keeler, recalls that Buzz was an "early hoarder." Keeler stated, "He never threw anything in that store away. It was always full of old feed sacks and egg cartons that he used for starting tomato seeds."

Sixteen-year-old Wanda Perrin
...on the night of her prom in 1946.
She was the love of Billy Harmon's life.

A young Kenny Harmon (Sad Papaw)
Pictured here second from the left. In order—Wanda Harmon, Kenny, Anita
Harmon, Paula Swinney, Nedra Swinney, and Nellie Harmon

An image of Peter and Mary's children, 1930-1931.
Uhel Harman passed away in December 1932. From Left: Matt and Ella
Stone Harmon, Frank and Nellie Lowback Harmon; Doc and Ella Frances
Gilliland Harmon; Curns Sr. and Idonia M. Avis Harmon, Uhel and Laura
Harman; Kendrick Cecil "KC" Harman; Lou Hall Harman.

Dona Harmon (the daughter of Curns Jr. and Lillian) is seated next to her cousin, Buzz Harmon (Doc Harmon's grandson).

Ella and Doc Harman.

Curns Harmon Sr.

Began the Harmon's Oklahoma watermelon legacy in Verden during the early1900's.

Doc and Ella's grandchildren
Buzz, Jim, Lucille, and Nellie.

Bobby Harmon,
The 2nd oldest child of Cecil and Edith Harmon.

93

Matt Harmon and his crew.

This is the threshing machine they used on the farm.

Floyd and Edna Harman, with their daughter, Lucille.

Elsie Harmon (daughter of Curns and Idonia) and Nellie Harmon (daughter of Floyd and Edna)

The twins, Curns and Cecil, were adorable babies.

A fun picture of the young twins,
Curns Gillis and Cecil Avis.

Doc's grandson, Buzz Harmon, owned the Dibble Crossroad Store. He is
pictured here with (his son) Wayne. (his wife) Mabel, and
his daughter, Anita (in the front).

Lizzy Harman Stone &Sam Stone, Lizzy was one of Babe's sisters.

Elsie Lillian Harmon Miller, Idonia Avis Harmon, and Velma Faye "Tootsie" Harmon Blalock.

Babe Harmon, Helen Harmon, and young Wayne Harmon posed outside Dibble Crossroad store. Helen is Cecil's oldest daughter.

Father and Son: Curns Sr and Cecil Harmon

Curns Jr. and his wife, Lillian owned a small café in Blanchard during the late 20's and early 30's.

During one of the winters through the Great Depression, a strong blizzard brought the town to a standstill. Though the Greyhound bus was able to make it to Blanchard, all other traffic was halted. The bus passengers spent several nights at their café, seeking warmth and protection from the storm. Friends and neighbors brought bedding and Curns and Lillian fed them at no cost. This was a time in America when no one thought twice about helping those in emergency situations.

Pictured here from August 1949, are Chief Harrison, his daughter, Cloma Harrison, Bill Harmon, Wanda Harmon, Faye Swinney (holding baby Paula Swinney), and Nedra Swinney standing in the front. At the time this photo was taken, Wanda Harmon was 4 months pregnant with her first child, Kenneth Layne Harmon. The baby would one day become known worldwide as—Sad Papaw!

Dona Harmon Pierce and Betty Jean Harmon Lancaster, Having fun with their puppies.

Elsie and Tootsie Harmon, the daughters of Curns and Idonia.

Glenn Harmon
Billy Harmon's cousin, his best friend – and partner in crime.

Jesse Harmon
The brother of Curns, Cecil, and Babe.

Paul McCorde
Babe Harmon's roommate in the military

Babe Harmon doing a 1-handed handstand. He was stationed away during World War I.

Mr. & Mrs. AC Cook with their daughters, Mellie and Nellie. In this photo, Nellie is only one year old.

*Babe Harmon and the exercise equipment he made from a sandbag, robes,
and a pulley for basic training for World War 1.*

SCHOOL DAYS 1946 · '47   SCHOOL DAYS 1945 · '46
Dibble High   Dibble High

Billy Harmon and Wanda Perrin.
This is Billy's senior picture; he is 18 years old.
Wanda is 16 years old in this class picture.

Billy Harmon
He was only 11 years old in this class picture.

Nellie Harmon during 1924.

*A picture of Nellie Harmon taken
in the early 1940's, around the
timethat she started teaching
Sunday School at Blanchard
Apostolic Church.*

*Babe Harmon in the late
1920's,near his farm in
Dibble.*

*Billy Harmon while he was visiting his
brother, Kenneth Swinney, in 1949, in
Whittier, California. Billy and Wanda
named their first child after him.*

104

Chapter 9

Journey to the West

May 1876

The years of heavy farm work had taken its toll on Peter. His body ached, and his health was failing. KC and Ellen had moved to Rock, Kansas a few years prior and upon hearing of his dad's condition, KC asked them to move closer to him. As KC was growing up, he watched his parents work tirelessly and sacrifice for him and his brothers and sisters. Now that they needed help, he wanted to be the one to step up for them. Throughout the years at Jellico Creek, all of the Harman children worked equally hard to help their parents though it was Peter and Mary who took on the brunt of the work. After numerous decisions and prayer, Peter and Mary accepted KC's offer and decided to move west.

Rock, Kansas was a fairly new community, only seven years old. MN Martindale established it in 1869. Martindale's home was the first building erected by European settlers in that area. Along with his log cabin, he planted 15 acres of corn and had 300 head of cattle. In the first year, they had a population of 160 people. The first school was built in Rock, in 1872. It was KC who would donate the land for the second schoolhouse to be built in 1882. It was named Rock Valley School. The school was rebuilt in 1896 on the east side of Rock Creek.

The first businesses to open in Rock were a post office, a blacksmith shop, wagon shop, stone quarry, and a grocery store. One of the storekeepers reflected how a general delivery included a carload of salt, a carload of flour and feed, 100 cases of quart fruit jars, ten (60 pounds) of Folgers coffee, 500 yards of outing (used to make clothes), and 100 pairs of rubber shoes.

It was early spring in 1877 when Peter and Mary set out on their long journey. They agreed to take turns driving the covered wagon. Uhel and his wife, Laura, traveled alongside in their wagon, with Lou and Frank riding in the back. Curns and Doc also drove a hitch with four cows attached.

Mary, Jaley, and Matt rode in the same wagon as their parents. To understand what Mary, Peter, and the Harman children were about to endure, this description was written by an anonymous traveler. The St. Joseph Missouri Gazette published his writing.

> *To enjoy such a trip ... a man must be able to endure heat like a Salamander, mud and water like a muskrat, dust like a toad, and labor like a jackass. He must learn to eat with his unwashed fingers, drink out of the same vessels as his mules, sleep on the ground when it rains, and share his blanket with vermin, and have patience with musketoes ... he must cease to think, except of where he may find grass and water and a good camping place. It is hardship without glory.*

Before the trip, they rubbed oil on the canvas cloth that covered the wagon to make it waterproof. It was tied shut on both ends to keep out the wind and the rain. On hot days, it was rolled open to catch the warm breeze. There were hooks inside the wagon to hand bonnets and jackets, cooking utensils, dolls, and guns.

They packed everything that was needed to start a new life in Kansas. The items they needed include clothes, hunting rifles, lanterns, sewing kits, tools, washbowls, medicine, first aid kit, soap, dishes, cups, the family Bible, silverware, pots & pans. The tools needed for the trip were an ax, shovel, hatchets, hammers and nails, anvil, grinding stone, animal traps, saws, knives, and rope. They were sure to carry plenty of blankets since, on the open plains, the air at night sometimes felt freezing. Sometimes, even during the day, they kept their legs covered with a blanket. To help the children pass the time, Mary packed dolls, jump ropes, marbles, and books.

Some of the food that they brought with them were crackers, eggs, bran, rice, cornmeal (10 pounds), flour (150 pounds), tea (10 pounds), coffee (100 pounds), bacon (40 pounds), oatmeal (10 pounds), vinegar (25 pounds), pickles (50 pounds), dried fruit (100 pounds), vegetables (5 pounds), dried beans (100 pounds), peas (100 pounds), dried beef (25 pounds), salt (50 pounds), sugar (50 pounds), and pork (5 pounds). Mary brought a cook box to store pepper, dried spices, and even molasses. And of course, there was also a barrel of water that weighed close to 350 pounds. There was more water found along the way. Coffee and tea masked the water's sometimes alkaline flavor.

They packed the bacon inside a barrel of bran to help it last longer. They packed eggs in the cornmeal, which then was used to make cornbread. There was plenty of cornbread to eat on the trip. It was inexpensive to make and traveled well. There were more uses for cornmeal. It was an ingredient in biscuits, gingerbread, and pie crusts.

For financial reasons, Peter and Mary also brought with them much-needed household items that could not easily be replaced. That list included:

- Rugs
- Stools
- Candles
- Coffee Grinder
- Bedding
- Dutch Oven
- Butter Churner
- Table and Chairs
- Wooden and Metal Buckets
- Butter Mold
- Rocking Chair
- Pitcher & Bowl
- Cooking Stove
- Cooking Utensils
- Spinning Wheel
- Farm Implements
- Seeds for Planting

The cows supplied fresh milk. On cold nights, Mary would prepare glasses of warm milk with cinnamon. The Harman children learned many tasks on these trips, such as: 1) how to identify and properly use different animals, flowers, and berries, 2) how to cook and live outdoors and fix broken things, and 3) how to skin and prepare buffalo and deer, and how to make beef jerky.

Mary also taught the children an interesting new way to make butter. They filled a pail halfway with milk and hung it from one of the wagons. The milk shook by the vibrations of going over the bumpy ground. A few hours later there were balls of butter in the pail.

Along the way, they hunted for food, repaired clothes, and searched for berries, honey, and vegetables. They covered their feet with the animal skins of the oxen. When their hooves grew tired and sore, they wrapped the animal skin around the bottom part of their legs and hooves. This was soothing for the oxen, helping them to feel much better. The unpredictable elements of the weather would be their biggest obstacle along the way. Rain would cause the ground to become a thick layer of mud, which in turn would cause the wagon wheels to sink and get stuck. To get unstuck, they layered grass in front of the wheels and pushed from behind while the oxen pulled. Peter also carried chains for the deep mud. On the other hand, if the ground was too dry, it kicked up so much dust that it got into their eyes and even aggravated the oxen. On the days when the dust in the air was too thick, they would have to stop and wait for it to settle. Hotter weather also brought on a greater need for water breaks for the animals.

There were several ruts carved into the ground from wagons traveling that same path. Hitting several of these ruts could cause the axles to break off of the wagon wheel, so they carried extras with them. The front and back wheels were different-sized axles. The front wheels were slightly smaller to make it easier to control the wagon when making turns. They carried an extra bucket of grease on a hook between the back wheels.

The trails were dotted with remnants of camping sites that were left behind by early travelers. Sadly, there were also a few grave markers from those who died trying to make the journey. Cholera, malaria, and high fevers took the lives of these men and women—and sometimes children.

The ride across the Great Plains was pretty slow. Peter and Mary could only travel 7-10 miles a day since each loaded wagon could weigh as much as 2,500 pounds. They knew it would take several months to reach Rock, so they planned for two stops along the way: one at Crawford County, Arkansas, and the other in Gallatin, Missouri. This would give Peter a much-needed rest. They deemed it necessary because they would arrive at these towns just as the winter weather was beginning to roll across the prairie.

Partway through the journey, they merged with a group of wagons also traveling west. It was commonly known as a wagon train. It was nice to talk to others about their journeys, their goals, and their ideas of the AMERICAN DREAM. There was an eclectic bunch of people traveling in the group with Peter and Mary. Along with the farmers, there were bakers, merchants, doctors, cooks, chimney sweeps, carpenters, blacksmiths, shoemakers, and teachers. Trail guides were stationed at the rivers to help travelers, like the Harman's, to get across safely. They used scows (large flat-bottomed boats) to carry the wagons across the water.

It was fascinating to follow the trails carved out by the wagons that traveled before them. These groups of wagons carried travelers of different nationalities, all in pursuit of a dream. Young people yearned to explore the open territories of the west and begin a new life. The families were looking for just the right place to plant the roots of their family trees. Then there were people like Peter and Mary, longing to reconnect with family members who traveled ahead of them. This was America, open, wild, and mysterious.

At noon, they stopped for a break and to eat lunch. This gave the children a chance to run and play and the animals a much-needed rest. The lunch stops lasted no more than an hour and a half; then it was time to move forward. When darkness fell across the prairie sky, the wagon train took a break for the night. The wagons formed a circle so that tents, beds, and campsites could be set up in the middle. During one of their stops, Mary traded some of her homemade bread for boxes of graham crackers. These were introduced to America a few years before and everyone in the family enjoyed them. Each morning, they would start back out pretty early. Their day began with a breakfast of cornbread, eggs, bacon, and strong black coffee. Then they hitched up their wagons and were back on the trail by 6:00 in the morning. During the trip, they often encountered Native American tribes, who for the most part, were friendly and wanted to trade with them. Not all of them were peaceful, but most were.

Almost four months after they left Kentucky, they reached Crawford County, Arkansas. Mary had family there, and they offered their homes for the Harman's to live with them. They stayed there for the winter. They did not have much farther to travel to reach Rock. So, by spring it was time to reload the wagons and continue their journey west.

It took a little less than two months for them to reach Gallatin. For young Doc Harman this would be more than rest from traveling. For it was while they were in Gallatin that he met and fell in love with Ella Frances Gilliland. They married on Monday, September 29, 1879. They walked down that aisle and swore before the eyes of God, and their friends and family, to cherish each other for the rest of their lives. This was precisely what they did. And it was here in Gallatin, Missouri that the Harman family tree would branch out into a new direction. A few days after Doc's wedding, Peter's health began to plummet. Mary didn't think he was strong enough to travel the rest of the way on the open bench of a covered wagon. She handed the reins over to Uhel's wife, Laura. She and Peter chose to take the stagecoach into Rock on the last leg of their trip. Sadly, Peter died just a few hours before they reached Rock. It was also his birthday. Peter turned 56 years old on the very day that he died.

In 1879, Ezra left Kentucky to join his family in Rock, Kansas. Since he was alone, he was able to travel on horseback. It made the trip easier and quicker. While he was crossing Indian territory in the newly established Oklahoma, he was attacked by Indians. He was shot with arrows, beaten, stripped naked, and whipped with straps and ropes. By a miracle, he was able to escape. When he reached Rock, Kansas, he was physically and mentally fatigued. His bruised body had barely healed wounds. He was also stricken with pneumonia. A few days after he arrived, he died with his family around him, on April 25, 1879.

Doc and Ella stayed in Missouri for 33 years. They toughed it out, as Peter taught Doc to do, all those years before in Kentucky. There were insect plagues, hot summers that would cut their crops short, intense thunderstorms, and hailstorms that rained down hail as big as hen eggs. One particular hailstorm left the stovepipe on the roof of their house flattened to the point that it was no thicker than a sheet of metal.

Her scariest experience happened in 1881 when a cyclone swooped in and ravaged the small town, they called home. Imagine a tight spiraling mass of clouds, formed in a circular shape. Ella was in the fields with her baby Homer when the cyclone erupted in the sky. She tried to make it all the way to the house but was unable to walk that far due to the high winds that traveled up to 70 miles an hour. All she could think to do was sit down with Homer on her lap and hold him tight, while she waited for it to pass. As she watched it destroy everything in its path, she expected to be blown away as it inched closer to her. Miraculously, the cyclone cloud jumped over her only to touch back down and destroy everything behind them. Moments later, it dissipated in the sky and the storm was over. She never forgot the events of that afternoon that almost claimed her life and Homer's.

~~~~ Journey Cakes ~~~~

Ingredients:
1 cup Milk
3 tbsp. Butter
1 tbsp. Molasses
1 pinch Salt
3 cups Cornmeal
½ cup Wheat Flour

- Place your milk in a saucepan, over low heat, to scald.
- Add the butter, molasses, and salt, and stir well.
- In a separate bowl, mix three cups of cornmeal and a half a cup of wheat flour. After the milk is heated, add it to the cornmeal and mix it well.
- Shape the dough into patties, about a half an inch thick and about 3 inches round.
- Fry them in a pan. Add butter to the pan if you are eating them right away.

Chapter 10

The Oklahoma Land Run
March 1889

On March 2, 1889, Congress signed into law the Oklahoma Land Rush of 1889. It allowed pioneers access to 20 million acres of land that was once a restricted territory. Once there, they had the opportunity to establish a homestead settlement claim. This was their chance to start a new life. The way it would work was that between March 2nd and April 22nd , the border would be guarded by US soldiers. This would give travelers time to prepare and make the journey to Oklahoma. At noon on the 22nd , access to the territory would be opened allowing travelers the opportunity to claim a piece of the land. This event later became known as the Run to Oklahoma.

Fed up with the flooding in Gallatin, Missouri, KC & Ellen, Uhel & Laura decided they wanted their families to be a part of the Americans ready to jump on the government's offer. Soon they packed up their wagons and set out on their next journey—the move to Oklahoma. By April 22nd, more than 50,000 travelers arrived at the Oklahoma border. They were nicknamed the Boomers. With excitement boiling over, the Harman's, alongside dozens of weary Americans, and even descendants of freed slaves, counted down the hours—then the minutes—to when they would crossover to Oklahoma soil and seize a chunk of the state that would soon be their own corner of the world. This became the home of many generations of Harman's. It would be years later when Uhel's son, Ted, would be elected mayor of Guthrie Oklahoma.

Then the time arrived! It was Monday at 11:50 AM, the morning of April 22nd. Soldiers called for everyone to get in line. They did the best they could, but it was not an easy task, given the multitude of people waiting at the border, some in covered wagons, some on horseback, and still, someone foot. In the middle of all the chaos were the Harman's, determined to make it into the new state. At noon, they fired a cannon, and the run into Oklahoma began. The end of the day reported hundreds of homestead claims.

On the downside from the events, many people claimed that some of the travelers snuck in earlier than the allowed day and time, nicknaming them the Sooners. Some of the battles between the Boomers and the Sooners turned bloody. A number of the Sooners were shot and killed. The courts became so congested with these claims of fraud that the government established a lottery system to settle all disputes and award claimed land accordingly. In the early 1900's Curns, Doc and Peter Frank moved their families to Verden, Oklahoma. Verden is 70 miles south of Cashion where KC and Uhel settled on April 22nd, 1889, during the Oklahoma Land Run.

Those who made Oklahoma their new home quickly earned the name Oklahomans. The state also earned the nickname, the Sooner State. The rich soil produced bumper crops of wheat, hay, cotton, and peanuts. This was the same year a dentist in Missouri started to promote peanut butter to his patients to fight bad breath. Peanut butter had been around for some time but not often used in cooking until now. After the release of peanut butter cookies came peanut butter & jelly sandwiches, also called Fancy Pants Sandwiches.

Fried food became a staple with Oklahomans, including fried pies, fried okra, calf fries (made from bull, pig, or sheep testicles), fried catfish, and their signature dish, Chicken Fried Steak. To make Chicken Fried Steak, they tenderized round pieces of steak and dipped them into a bowl of milk and eggs that were beaten together, remembering to flip it over and cover it entirely. The next step was to place it in a flour mixture. This contained flour, cayenne, black pepper, and a variety of spices chosen by the cook. Each family made it their own way. They fried it on both sides until golden brown. That was the fried chicken part. They poured gravy on top that they made by mixing the grease with flour and milk. It was cooked until the consistency of the gravy was complete.

Oklahoma soon had their first outbreak. It was Texas Fever that contaminated hundreds of people across Verden and neighboring towns. Many of the Harman children were among those who fell ill. The fever brought on a cough, fever, chills, sneezing, fatigue, headaches and earaches, muscle pain, and trouble breathing. It could last up to three weeks. At the time, there was a cattle trail that led from Texas through Oklahoma, Missouri, and Kansas. The longhorn cattle were infected with the fever by ticks. As they grazed the farms on the journey through Oklahoma, the ticks began to infect the other livestock on the farm. It was so bad that by 1894, the cattle trails closed completely. Kansas even banned Texas Longhorns from their state.

Starting new farms in Oklahoma did not help them to escape the damage that Mother Nature could hammer down on the crops. A brutally hot summer cut the crops short in 1894. Even the vegetables in the garden struggled to grow through the dry soil and the searing summer heat.

As the Harman children grew to experience the world on their own, each one met and fell in love at a young age. As they had their children, the Harman family tree flourished across the western territory.

Mary stayed in Arkansas until 1894; then she decided to move closer to Doc and Ella, who lived in Birmingham, Missouri. They all moved to Blue Springs, Missouri, in 1904. Later that year, they moved once more, to join their family in Verden, Oklahoma. In 1909, when Mary was visiting her son Peter, she fell ill with pneumonia. Unable to fight it off, Mary died several weeks later on February 7, 1909.

KC Harman

KC was now 37 years old and a strong family man in his own right. He had a farm of his own and was a leader in the Rock, Kansas community. It was only a year before that he donated land for the town to build their second schoolhouse. He and other men in town even helped to build it. When KC was 21 years old, and after he and Ellen had been married for only nine months, she gave birth to their first child, a son, whom they named Ed Harman. He was born October 12, 1867.

They next welcomed three daughters into the world. Elva Harman was born five years later on October 27, 1872. Mary Gertrude Harman was born July 14, 1876. It was three years later on August 8, 1879, when their third daughter, Emma Matilda Harman, was born. It wasn't until five years later, on August 23, 1884, that John Harman was born. Sadly, John would not reach adulthood. He died on August 19, 1896, just a few days shy of his

12th birthday. In 1877, their last child, a son, died when he was only a few days old.

Liz Harman

Liz was married to Joe Ryan, Sr. shortly before the family left Kentucky. They had two children together. Joe Ryan, Jr. was born on January 10, 1868. Their daughter, Mary Ryan, was born two years later. She was the first granddaughter named after Mary. Liz and Joe's marriage was short-lived and ended on quiet terms. She later married Tony Smith. They did not have children as a couple.

Uhel Harman

When Uhel was 25 years old, he met Laura Ann Smith of Guthrie Oklahoma. She was a quiet young lady whom he courted for nearly a year before he proposed to her. The couple had eight children through the years. Their first son, Theodore "Ted" Harman was born September 17, 1879. Ted grew up to serve several terms on the town council before being elected the mayor. In his early 40's, he went to work for the State Capital Printing Company. After several years of learning every aspect of the printing business, he bought the company out and renamed it the Co-Operative Publishing Company. They had two more sons, Benjamin Franklin Harman (born March 26, 1882) and Joseph William Harman (born January 31, 1886). Laura then gave birth to five daughters. Her first daughter, Rebecca, died at birth. Their daughters born after Rebecca were Bessie "Bell" Harman (January 30, 1889), Gertrude May Harman (July 26, 1890), Grace Pearl Harman (February 14, 1893), and Maude Fay Harman (August 26, 1895).

Curns Harman

Curns married Jennie Creech, in 1877, when he was 22 years old. Curns and Jennie had five children together. Their first son, James (Jim) Harman, was born in 1878. Lula Harman was born in 1881, and two years later, Jennie gave birth to Elizabeth (Lizzy) Independence Harman. She was given the name "Independence" because she was born on the Fourth of July. She then gave birth to two sons, Jesse Gillis Harman, born April 12, 1885, and William (Babe) Harman, born on December 3, 1887.

Sadly, Jennie died from complications from pneumonia in 1902. Jesse and Babe were seven and five years old. Though Curns and Jennie had a close marriage, he knew that he would not be able to raise his boys alone. It was two years after her death that he traveled to New York to meet a mail-order bride, Idonia.

Curns had five more children with Idonia. Their oldest daughter, Margaret, was only a toddler when she died in 1908. On February 22, 1909, she gave birth to twins, Curns Gillis and Cecil Avis. Their next child was a daughter, Elsie Lillian Harman. Their youngest daughter, Velma (Tootie) Faye Harman was born on December 26, 1915.

Horatio "Doc" Gates Harman

Doc was 20 years old when he became a father. Ella gave birth to Homer Harman on October 17, 1880. Their daughter, Annie Mae Harman, was born November 1, 1881. Lula Harman was born two years later on January 11, 1883. Sadly, Lula died when she was only two years old, on March 4, 1885. Their next daughter, Pearl Della Harman, was born on November 20, 1884. Tragedy struck the family four months later when two-year-old Lula died on March 4, 1885.

Pearl wandered away from home when she was two years old and got lost. Ella searched all over but could not find her. In the distance, she spotted a wagon that suspiciously appeared to be circling in the grass. Little did she know it was Doc. He happened to hear a baby crying and stopped to look around, and it was Pearl. He was not even aware of the fact that his baby girl wandered away. The prairie grass was taller than Pearl, well over her head, causing her to get lost quickly and easily.

Ella had three more children after this. Floyd Thompson Harman was born on August 8, 1889. Their youngest son, Horatio Peter Harman, was born February 10, 1894. They nicknamed him, "Raish." Their youngest daughter, Ruth Gilliland Harman was born on August 16, 1903.

Louraney (Lou) Harman

Lou was 22 years old when she married Patterson Hall on November 7, 1883. Three years later on September 20, 1886, she had her first baby, Alma Rachel Hall. Her next three children were all daughters, Mary Serelda

Hall (January 25, 1888), Florence May Hall (October 21, 1888), and Lula Edna Hall (June 8, 1891). Florence was only 23 years old when she died.

Their next child was a son, Arthur Ray Hall, born on June 15, 1893. He died shortly before he turned three years old, on June 4, 1896. Their daughter, Edith Vivian Hall, was born on November 13, 1899. She also died when she was only a toddler. Their youngest son, Charles Patterson Hall was born on July 4, 1903.

Mary Serelda Harman

Mary was married to Reuben White, and together they had four children, Myrtle, Grace, Lloyd, and Mary. Reuben worked for the newly formed Singer Sewing Machine Company. Mary was extremely close to her younger sister, Jaley. The two of them were even married to brothers. Both ladies had a passion for writing and often wrote letters to each other. They shared recipes and news, both good and bad, such as the ongoing problem that Mary had with her neighbor's chickens tearing up her garden.

Peter Frank Harman

Peter became an ordained Baptist Minister. He and his wife, Nellie, planted numerous churches that continue to serve their communities today. The couple had nine children together: Mary Elizabeth (Betty) Harman (December 22, 1889), Zenith Celard (November 8, 1891), Peter Pearly (February 28, 1900), Zelma Lowback (November 27, 1903), Gladys Nell (September 8, 1905), Clarence (Snowball) Richard (July 10, 1908), Paul Frank (September 3, 1910), Howard Gaines (January 23, 1913), and their youngest child, Genevia Harman, was born on September 30, 1916. Sadly, Zenith died shortly before her seventh birthday.

Jaley Ellen Harman

Jaley married Charles White in 1885 when she was 17 years old. It was Charles' brother, Reuben, who was married to her sister, Mary. Their first child was a daughter named Gertrude, nicknamed Gerty. She was born in 1886. Five years later, she gave birth to a son. Sadly, at the time of his birth, she fell ill from consumption (now called tuberculosis). Consumption took a heavy toll on Jaley. She suffered from high fevers, chills, flushing of the cheeks, weight loss, chest pains, and weakness. She developed a violent cough, often bringing up phlegm and blood. A cough also made it difficult for her to breath. She was not sure how she contracted consumption. All she knew for certain was that she was, at one time, near someone who coughed or sneezed. She died on Wednesday, May 20, 1891. Their son died a few months after Jaley passed away.

Gerty went to live with her Aunt Mary when her mother died. She stayed with her for two years. During that time, her father met and married Florence Hall. The new couple then went back to pick up Gerty. From there, Charles moved the family to Indiana. Though Charles was grateful for Mary's help during that rough patch of his life, after the move, Mary lost all contact with her niece.

William Madison (Matt) Harman

Matt married Louella Stone on January 15, 1893, and the couple had five children together: Ernest Earl (March 15, 1894), Ethel Edith (September 5, 1898), Leah Lydell (January 15, 1900), Leona Maybelle (December 27, 1903), and Eugene Dale (October 24, 1908).

It was Matt's grandson, Bill Harman, who was the first to change the spelling of the family name from HARMAN to HARMON. After he had a falling out with several family members, he said he no longer wanted to be a member of the family. He changed the spelling of his last name and moved his family to Oklahoma. The family members who followed him also changed their last name to be spelled with an O, and to date, the name change has stayed with them—HARMON.

As the family divided, from the events of the feud, those who moved on to Dibble and Blanchard changed the spelling of their name to HARMON. The others continued spelling their name HARMAN.

Curns' daughter, Lula, and her husband opened a bakery in Blanchard, Oklahoma. The bakery was a popular stop for families during the 1920's.

~~~~ Old Fashioned Peanut Butter Cookies ~~~~

Ingredients:
2 Large Eggs
2 Cups Flour
2 teaspoons Baking Soda
½ teaspoon Salt
1 Cup Peanut Butter
½ Cup Butter, softened
1 Cup firmly packed Brown Sugar
1 Cup White Sugar
½ Cup Crisco
1 teaspoon Vanilla

- Preheat the oven to 350 degrees.
- Cream together the sugars, Crisco, and peanut butter.
- Add the eggs and vanilla.
- Sift the dry ingredients together and add gradually until blended well.
- Bake for 10-12 minutes.

*You can press a crisscross pattern on each cookie with fork tines to cook it thoroughly. The original recipe did not call for this.

Chapter 11

————◆●●◆————

Curns Family

Farm October 1905

A new generation brought exciting changes to the country. Almost half the homes in America had telephones installed. Curns was one of those to include a home telephone for his family. It was a dry cell battery-powered phone and had to be hand-cranked to make a call. His telephone number was "20, ring 3," which meant three short rings. The crank was turned 1 and ½ half times to dial the operator to make a call.

Children were clamoring for the new Crayola Crayons. Aspirin took the place of codeine on medicine shelves. The newest sweet treats that Americans longed for were glass bottles of Coca-Cola, the Hershey Bar, and Tootsie Rolls. The Ford Model T was clanking up and down city roads, bringing with it a barrage of new traffic laws, including a speed limit of 10 miles an hour. A year earlier, the government started issuing license plates to monitor the cars that were hitting the streets; before that, people made their own license plates. The Harmons used birthdays, lucky numbers, and initials for the license plates that they created.

Families were going to theaters to see their favorite actors in silent films, such as Charlie Chaplin, Mary Pickford, and Lillian Gish. The popular movie playing was The Kleptomaniac, starring Aline Boyd. People were enjoying Jack London's book, Call of the Wild. The Boston Cooking School Cookbook was published, changing the way women cook because their recipes were noted as listing the ingredients first and then the directions below them. Before that, they wrote recipes in paragraph form without listing exact measurements. Children were reading The Wonderful Wizard of Oz, published in 1900 by L. Frank Baum. It was reprinted two years later under the name, The Wizard of Oz. Peter Rabbit, the popular children's book of all time was self-published in 1901. A year later it was picked up by Frederick Warne & Company. Lucy Maud Montgomery released Anne of Green Gables in 1908. Scottish author, J. M. Barrie, wrote Peter Pan in 1911. A significant fact about Peter Pan was that the book created the name, "Wendy."

In 1903, baseball fans across the country witnessed the first World Series. The Harmons were indeed a part of that crowd. They were playing baseball since 1846 when the game was first brought over to America. And in 1903, they listened to the first World Series. It was the Pittsburgh Pirates vs. the Boston Americans (later known as the Boston Red Sox). The Americans beat the Pirates, winning five out of nine games. The following year, much to the disappointment of baseball fans, the World Series was canceled. When it was determined that the winner of the National League was the New York Giants and the winner of the American League was the New York Islanders (later known as the Yankees), the coaches and players began to butt heads over territorial claims. The Giants felt that the Islanders were trying to invade as New York's baseball team. They refused to play against each other. Officials had to step in and settle the feud. The wanted the World Series to be a yearly game played for many decades to come. They hated to see the idea come to an end over a territorial spat. Now that the dust had settled, it was time for players to take to the fields once more. This World Series would come down to the New York Giants vs. the Philadelphia Athletics. There was no doubt about it; baseball had grown to be as American as apple pie. Americans also witnessed the first Rose Bowl, played in Pasadena, California on January 1, 1902. The Michigan Wolverines beat Stanford University 49-0.

Curns was also feeling the winds of change. He and his children were now spelling their Harmon name with an "O." His first wife, Jennie, passed away from pneumonia in 1902. After Jennie's death, the family was quarantined for 30 days. The truant officer, who also worked as the Health Officer, nailed a cardboard sign to the front door that read, "No Visitors." When the 30 days was up, he removed the sign. Curns and the children had to leave the house while he fumigated it by burning large sulfur candles in a shallow pan. After several hours, the windows and doors were opened to admit fresh air so the family could re-enter safely.

It had been three years since Jennie's death. Their oldest son, Jim, was now 27 years old. His daughter, Lula, was married and living in Blanchard, with her husband, also named Jim, and they had just opened a bakery in town. They delivered baked goods to people's homes and often pushed handcarts through the parks to sell their treats.

Their daughter, Elizabeth (Lizzy) was born on the Fourth of July, so they gave her the middle name "Independence." She was also newly married to Samuel Cravens Stone. Their youngest two sons were Jesse Gilllis (now 20 years old) and William (Babe) Harmon, 18 years old. Each of the boys left school after third grade to work on the farm. The girls also left school early to work inside the home.

Oklahoma was ideal for farming. The soil was rich and full of nutrients which is just what a farmer needs. Yet, Mother Nature still had her stages where she was unkind to farmers. The Oklahoma summers were at times blistering hot, bringing long droughts with them. The bitter winter storms would bite down and often rain hailstones that mimicked the winter storms that Curns and his brothers battled against in Kentucky. The smothering force of the hail once cut Curns' chimney into pieces, as if an ax had been taken to it.

Farming equipment was also making great strides. The farming tools used by Curns were mostly small handheld pieces. One of the larger pieces was the cultivator. It was a horse-drawn plow with six blades. This was used to dig furrows to plant seeds. A flail was used to separate the seeds from the other particles of the grain. Curns had to be extremely careful with these types of tools. He knew of farmers who lost limbs and even their lives by incorrect use of these tools. One little slip could cause a gash that would quickly bring on an infection. One of the major developments was the combine, a tool that could cut and thresh a field of grain at the same time. The invention of the steel plow was also an asset. It had sharper blades that could cut through the thick prairie roots. Another essential tool for Curns and his brothers was the reaper, a device that could cut grain better than the scythe.

In the business world, farmers were greatly taken advantage of on a regular basis. On more than one occasion, Curns found himself under the ruling thumb of greedy businessmen. As his farm grew, Curns would often need new machinery and fertilizer. Since a farmer's wages were quite meager during planting season, he was forced to borrow the money to purchase the items. When the weather or insects destroyed his crops, he found himself hopelessly in debt. The railroads were charging Curns and his farming neighbors more to ship their products than what the buyer was willing to pay. Because of this, he had to turn his attention to the community for the bulk of his sales.

Sadly, there was no one in Washington looking out for the farmers, and congress ignored their pleas for help. Farmers began to organize into groups called Granges and Farmers Alliances. They launched a political group called the Peoples Party, also known as the Populists, running one for president in 1892. They did manage to elect four state governors and 5 US senators. Curns and his brothers were all a part of the alliances.

The ringer washer was another modern improvement for the home. The ringer washer rescued the Harmon women from the drudgery of the washboard. It was started by using your foot to engage a flywheel. It did not always start right away. There were some days that it would not start at all, and it was back to using the washboard. A gasoline engine could be added to the ringer washer for easier starting. The clothes were rung by hand operated rollers attached to the tub and hung out to dry. Though the farm was making great strides, there was still something missing at home.

Curns was not one for wanting to spend the rest of his years alone. So, in 1905, he traveled to New York to meet a mail-order bride named Idonia Avis. While he was in New York, he was able to observe the Statue of Liberty, a gift from France that was given to America only 20 years earlier, in 1885. Curns and Idonia had an instant connection and spent the rest of their lives devoted to each other.

Curns was a peculiar man. He carried a saltshaker with him and put salt on everything—even ice cream. One of Curns' favorite dishes that Idonia was great at preparing for the family was Kentucky's famous Chess Pie. It was a favorite of Curns' from his years at Jellico Creek.

Soon, Curns and Idonia had children together. Their first daughter, Margaret Harmon was born in 1908. She died when she was only a few days old. But the couple was blessed a year later with twins! They named them Curns Gillis Harmon and Cecil Avis Harmon. Their next child was a daughter that they named Elsie Lillian Harmon. Their youngest child was born on Saturday, December 26, 1915—a daughter they named Velma Faye

Harmon. They gave her the nickname Tootie.

In 1912, Doc moved closer to Curns, and those two worked together harvesting a peach crop. Every year they sent 1000 bushels of peaches to market. Considering that there are 150 peaches in a bushel, that means they sold 150,000 peaches a year.

Curns' son, Babe, joined the ranks of thousands of men across America and left home in 1918 to serve in World War I. He was stationed in France and was on his way to the front line when his platoon received the announcement that the war was over. He served out his years in the army, and when his military service was complete, he returned to Oklahoma. There he stayed nearby his father's home, and they helped each other on their farms.

Raish followed his dad, Doc, and moved to Blanchard in 1917. Blanchard was an exciting new addition to Oklahoma, having only been established ten years prior, in 1907, by the Canadian Valley Construction Company. In its first year, Blanchard had sprung to life, becoming home to 40 businesses, including a state and national bank, four blacksmith shops, three livery barns, two-grain elevators, and a weekly newspaper, The Blanchard Record. Art and Bill Blanchard opened a post office and the first general store in town. By 1910, 629 people were living in Blanchard. The first graduating class of Blanchard's school marched across the stage in 1915. It was only two years later that Raish and Doc moved to the small bedroom community with a handful of seeds and dream in their heart of growing their family there. They started a small farm together that grew through the years and became known as Shady Nook. They would both be shocked and pleasantly surprised to see that farm still in full operation 90 years later.

Blanchard, Oklahoma had since swelled in population and in pride as they struggled to preserve the history of the town that was started by a team of travelers.

~~~~ Chess Pie ~~~~

Ingredients:
1 Whole Egg (room temperature)
2 Egg Yolks (room temperature)
1 tsp. Vinegar
2 Tbsp. Flour
2 Tbsp. Water
1 Cup Sugar
1 Stick Butter (melted and cooled)
1 8" Pie Shell

- Preheat oven to 375 degrees.
- Place eggs and yolks in a bowl.
- Mix until well-blended but not foamy.
- Mix water and vinegar. Stir in eggs.
- Mix flour and sugar together.
- Slowly add liquid mixture; mix well with wooden spoon.
- Add cooled, melted butter and stir until well-mixed.
- Pour into pie shell and bake for 30 minutes.

Chapter 12

Dibble, Oklahoma
1923

Two loves that Babe Harmon inherited from his family bloodline were farming and baseball. Like his uncles before him, the game became his prime source of enjoyment during the spring and summer months. In 1919, the Black Sox scandal threatened the future of Major League Baseball. It turned away many fans who were disappointed in their players who had sunk so low, all in an effort to help gamblers reap thousands of dollars, bringing the phrase, "Say it isn't so, Joe," to the lips of baseball fans across the country. Sandlot baseball became very popular. Sandlot teams consisted of players as young as teens and men in their 40's! Babe organized his first sandlot team in the 1930's. His last team played in the late 1940's. One of Babe's players was his younger brother Cecil, 21 years younger. Cecil used a homemade bat that was so heavy most players couldn't effectively swing it. One former teammate said, "no sandlot player I saw could hit a ball farther than Cecil Harmon!" In the 1950's sandlot became "Little League" and that which was formerly known as sandlot baseball became "outsiders' baseball". Sadly, outsiders ball began to lose its popularity in the late '50's and early '60's. Just when I was almost old enough to play, the many years of sandlot/outsider baseball ended!

Babe Harmon chose to grow his family home in Dibble, Oklahoma. The town was named for brothers, James and John Dibble, though there was no exact record showing when Dibble became a community. Many believe that Dibble was established in 1894 because that was when they opened their first post office. The first postmaster was Horatio Orem. The post office closed between 1926—1953. In 1901, during the turn of the century, Dibble grew to include 100 residents, a hotel, a grocery store, a general store, a blacksmith, a doctor, and three stockmen people who looked after livestock. Farming remained the primary source of business to residents. In 1906, the Oklahoma Central Railway, which was supposed to extend through Dibble, changed direction and moved north to Blanchard instead. Because of that, the town lost many of its established businesses. It only lasted a short time. New companies grew where the old ones left. By 1911, there were 150 residents, a new confectioner (selling candy and desserts), two general stores, a blacksmith, a doctor, and a drugstore. By 1918, the population dropped to 125, yet the business district continued to grow to include a gristmill (a mill that grinds grain into flour), a cotton gin, and a feed store.

Babe married Nellie Harrison Swinney in 1923. Nellie had been married twice before meeting Babe. She had two children when they met. They were two sons, 11-year-old named Aurelius Ward Harrison and 5-year-old Harold Kenneth Swinney. Her first husband was a Native American who left 160 acres of Indian land to her. She and her sons were living in a small home on that land. Babe was proud to raise them as his own. On Friday, August 31, 1928, the two welcomed the first and only child they would have together. A son they named WB Billy Harmon Jr. was born.

Their son, Billy, was a mischievous child who always had to be on the roam. When he sat still too long, he got bored. And when he got bored, he got into trouble. One of Billy's earliest memories was when his mother found him standing in front of the mirror with tears streaming down his face. He explained to his worried mother, "I just found out that I have freckles and I don't like them."

In the late 1920's Babe began selling produce to stores. Watermelons, cantaloupes, tomatoes, okra and other produce were also sold on the streets, which was known as peddling. Blanchard was Babe's favorite place to do his peddling.

Sadly, in 1932 Babe started suffering terribly from ulcers. This confined him to bed rest for most of 1933. It was incredibly frustrating for Babe. He spent his life working from sun-up to sun-down. He grew disappointed in himself for not being able to get back to work which probably did not help with his ulcers. He also started growing stir crazy and had to think of creative ways to pass the time. His favorite cat often jumped on his bed to check on him, so Babe came up with a game to play with his little buddy. He tied a button to a long piece of string, then he would toss the button across the room, and tug slowly on the string to reel the button back. They played this game for countless hours.

His 5-year-old son, Billy, would sometimes pop into his bedroom to visit him. They had an arm-wrestling game where Babe would hold one arm in the air and chide Billy by saying, "Try and pull my arm down." With the help of Dr. White of Oklahoma City, Babe made a full recovery. Babe would buy melons in Texas and sell them to grocery stores in Oklahoma City and to the public in Blanchard. He purchased a '34 Chevy and took the back seat out so that he could use it to haul their crops. It also served as their produce stand in town and on the side of the road. They even sold vegetables to Oklahoma City restaurants. They fed the corn stalks to the cows and pigs. Generations of Harmon men would continue to sell produce in Oklahoma City for over 40 years.

Billy also had the job of carrying a bucket to the creek to get water for the cows. After 1937, they had a pump installed near the house, so he no longer had to carry water from the creek. During the winter months the cattle were kept in 2 feedlots, one lot was for the cows and the other lot was for the older calves.

Times were extremely difficult for most farmers. Several years prior, in 1931, a severe drought swept across America, hitting the western states particularly hard, devastating the Great Plains. After four years of the same unrelenting drought, the grassy plains and hillsides completely dried up. Without the grass to serve as an anchor against the high winds, the stale hot air kicked up dirt from the dry, cracked topsoil and formed billowing clouds of dust called black blizzards. They swirled across the farms, coating the crops in thick dust causing them to wither and dry-up. Farmers watched helplessly as their crops blew away. These dust clouds also caused the cattle to choke. There were so many black blizzards that the era became known as the Dirty 30's.

In spite of the Great Depression, the severe drought, and those nasty dust clouds (dust storms), Babe continued to prosper with his farm. He was even able to afford to hire help for their 400 acres of farmland. Nellie also cooked meals for the help. Nellie was a praying wife and mother and

128

belonged to a Help Meet, which was similar to a prayer/support group. The family credited his success through the years to hard work on Babe's side mixed with the power of prayer. During the 1940's, Nellie's strong religious beliefs grew as she and the family attended the Apostolic Church in Blanchard. The church was formed in 1938 by Cecil Lambert (who had worked for Babe on the Harmon homestead), Gene Richey, Tom Richey, Sly Richey, Grover Andrews, and Ed Wayland. Nellie was a Sunday school teacher there for part of the 1940's. The church was later named Trinity Free Holiness. To this day, the Harmons continue to represent in the Blanchard Trinity Free Holiness.

The black blizzards continued to creep across the farmer's fields. During the worst dust storms, the sky would darken for days. Up to 38 of these massive dust storms were reported in 1933 alone. Because of the severity of the situation, Franklin Roosevelt established the Emergency Farm Mortgage Act which granted $200 million to farmers. This allowed them to refinance their mortgage so they would not lose their farms. By the end of 1934, 75% of the country was in a drought. In 1935, the cattle that were deemed unfit for human consumption were bought by the government's Cattle Buying Program, for $14-20 per head.

Farmers, like Babe, soon found themselves battling another enemy—grasshoppers. Since grasshoppers thrive in dry weather, they came in like massive swarms. They would blanket the farms and ate the crops that were not destroyed by the drought. In hours, they would devour entire fields of crops. They loved the taste of salt and would bite people to eat holes in their clothes and chew on horse drawn equipment just for the salt that was created from sweating. So many were run over by cars that they left the streets slick. Often, trains could not travel uphill because the tracks were greased from the grasshopper's bodies.

April 14, 1935 was the most devastating day of the Dirty 30's. Billy was 6 1/2 years old that day. He and his father were on the porch, looking out across the fields, when they saw a massive dark cloud slowly rolling in from the Northwest. At first, they were happy about it. Feeling a form of relief wave over him, Babe sighed and told Billy, "It will be stormin' after a while!" It was a storm alright but much worse than rain. It was something they never expected—it was solid DUST. This dust storm paled in comparison to the black blizzards that they had been experiencing. Some of the clouds that day rose as high as 10,000 feet, and they extended all the way to New York City. This day would go down in history as Black Sunday. Dirt from the crushing dust storm found its way into their home from the cracks around the windows and door frames. Nellie hung wet sheets in the windows to block out as much dust as possible. Her neighbors felt the same panic as they tried to block out the dust that was fighting its way inside their homes. Nellie was cooking dinner when the dust exploded over Oklahoma. She had to cover the food and plates with a sheet until everyone came inside to eat. By the end of the day, and for weeks afterward, even the most well-sealed homes were covered with a layer of dust. Many people wore dust masks when they had to go into town or out to work. And children wore them to school. By December, they determined that 850,000,000 tons of topsoil had blown off the prairie that day.

No relief was in sight. The dust blew for eight years leaving a yellowish-brown haze that lingered in the air. By 1939, the drought came to an end, as the skies across the country cracked open releasing a down pouring of rainstorms. Within weeks, the dry rolling hills were plush green.

At home, Nellie continued to look for ways to keep Billy busy. Since his brothers were older than he, Billy did not have anyone to play with at home. That was until his cousin, Glenn, moved a half a mile away. Glenn was the son of Babe's brother, Jesse. The two quickly became best friends and were inseparable. Nellie always knew where to find Billy—at Glenn's house. He was there all day, every day. Billy's parents would pick him up each night. Nellie tried to get Billy to stay closer to home and play by himself, but he would not do it. She once got so frustrated that she tied him to the front porch post. He was able to sweet talk his mom into believing that he would not run off if she untied him. So, she unraveled the rope. As she was turning around, before the rope hit the ground, Billy darted off in the direction of Glenn's house.

On other days she sent Billy to the yard to play with explicit directions to stay nearby. He still devised yet another plan to get away—one that took her several weeks to figure out. In front of their house was the main road in town. It was unpaved, and there were long and deep ruts on both sides that were carved out by cars and wagons. Billy would drop to his stomach and wriggle up the path of the grooves, keeping out of sight of his mother. Then when he knew the coast was clear, he bound to his feet and took off once more.

Billy and Glenn went to the movies every Saturday. They were especially excited when the Lone Ranger movies were airing. He was their hero, so naturally, one of their favorite games to play was Cowboys & Indians. They tried to mimic their idol but were a little off on the words, shouting, "Hi! Ho! Silver! Get Going," instead of "Hi! Ho! Silver! Away!" When Billy became an adult one of his favorite stories was one day, he rode his stick horse to school, and someone took it, so he had to walk home!

Billy and Glenn were 6 and 7 years old and could stir up trouble quicker than the villains being chased by the Lone Ranger and Tonto. One afternoon, they came across a skyrocket that was left behind from the Fourth of July picnic and wanted to light it, but it was not dark enough outside yet. They decided that the cellar seemed to be good and dark, so they went there to light it, shutting the door behind them. They stuck the skyrocket under the crack of the door and lit the fuse. It flew into the air, looped around, and knocked a chunk of concrete out of the wall on impact. The crashing and buzzing sound were so loud that it alerted Billy's Aunt Lucile who came running to check on them.

Five years later, Jesse and his wife separated. For several months after the separation, Glenn moved back and forth between their homes. When he was 13 years old, he moved in with his dad for good.

Since Billy, (with Glenn's help), had been labeled a troublemaker, it was easy for the teachers to blame him when things went wrong in class. During one of his study halls, the teacher, Miss Patton, left the class alone to retrieve items from a nearby room. Her classroom quickly turned into an uproar as students were laughing loudly and throwing paper balls. Miss Patton was furious! She stormed into the room and marched directly to Billy. Using him as an example, she grabbed him by the hair, lifted him up from his chair, and began to scold him and the others.

Billy was 13 years old when his big brother, Kenneth, was drafted and left home to fight in World War II. Babe also traveled that route. He served the military during World War I after being drafted. When Kenneth returned home, he rarely talked about the war. The family respected that choice and did not pepper him with questions. All Billy knew for sure was that something left Kenneth with an injury to his legs. And for the rest of his life, Kenneth had trouble walking. As a teenager, Billy was still full of energy all day. He was still not a good listener. Once, Babe was on the south side of the house shelling corn, and he told Billy that he needed his help. Billy casually scoffed back with a NO. Babe gave him that angry stare. He stood up as Billy began running. Babe threw an ear of corn that hit him in the back of the head and knocked him smooth out. Nellie panicked at the sight of Billy on the ground. You can say Babe's baseball arm came in handy that day. And Billy had a lasting reminder of why he should never say NO when his dad told him to do something.

Soon Billy found a new way to vent his bottled-up energy and started playing basketball and baseball. And then he discovered girls. Billy was 15 years old when he met his "first true love," a 13-year-old girl named Joyce Adams. He was always afraid of girls, and he dated Joyce for three months before he tried to kiss her. He was scared to try it sooner because he did not want her to get mad at him.

In high school, he met Wanda Lee Perrin. The two first met because they rode the bus together. For Billy, it was love at first sight. The two dated throughout high school. A week after she graduated, they got married. They were first married at the courthouse. However, at the end of the service, they were told the marriage would not be legal because she was underage. Even though she was only two years younger than Billy, she still needed a written consent letter from her parents that was notarized. This was on a Friday afternoon and the notaries were closed. They traveled back home and explained to Wanda's parents what they had done. Bright and early Saturday morning, they all went to a notary to get the letter. Afterward, they went to the sheriff's office to get help with their marriage because the Justice of the Peace office was now closed. He was able to track down a judge who met them at the bank building where the Justice of the Peace office was located on the second floor. On May 22, 1948, after two days—and two weddings— they were officially married.

That day, they moved in with Billy's parents. This was a temporary stay, while they got their house fixed and ready to move in to. Shortly before the house was ready, on Thursday, January 12, 1950, Wanda gave birth to the couple's first child—a son they named Kenneth Layne Harmon. When Kenny was a year old, their house, up the hill from Billy's parents, was ready for them.

Later that year, the family stepped out to the movies, and within those few short hours, a fire broke out reducing their home to rubble and ash. They were never able to pinpoint the direct cause of the fire, but they believed it was either from the coal stove or the lantern lamp that was left burning. The family was forced to move into an old potato house. It was a small building that was 40 feet long and 20 feet wide. It had a cement floor and walls made out of clay tile. There was no inside ceiling, just the outside roof. Fortunately, it did have electric lights. There was also a 50-gallon barrel heater, refrigerator box, and a kerosene stove. From there, they bought a 3-room house. But in that home, there was no running water, and they did not have enough money to build a water line. Because of this, they had to haul water from Billy's parents' house in 10-gallon cans. They had a pick-up truck to haul the cans but had to make several trips to complete the task. They stayed there temporarily and bought a new, larger home in 1964. This home was exciting for Billy and Wanda for it had running water, electricity, and a washer & dryer set. It was a treasure for a growing country family in the early 1960's.

Wanda soon went on to work for Western Electric where she made parts for telephones. She stayed with them for 31 years as a line operator. About ten years into her career, Billy was also hired to work in the same department. But being a country boy, he was becoming restless once again. He was used to long days in the open air. Now he was stuck inside a factory where the only signs of outside life shone through a small window on the other side of the room. After three months, he went to Wanda and explained that he just could not do it anymore. He told her that he felt like he was going to lose his mind standing in one spot all day inside a factory. She understood. The next day, he was back on the farm, working with his dad.

In the late 1950's, Billy began planting two types of melons together in hopes of creating a new type of melon that would carry the best qualities from each one. It worked! It was a Cobb Jim-Black Diamond cross. One of them weighed in at 102 pounds. Figuring the years that Babe grew melons on his family's farm, and now on his own farm with his son, Billy, they realized that together they had been growing melons for over 80 years.

You could say that Billy and Wanda had a relationship just as dedicated and loving as Mary and Peter had so many years before in Kentucky. The Harmon men were always loyal and loving to their wives and their children. There were years when they were not able to give their children much in possessions, but one thing was certain: they provided good food and a lot of love. Wanda became famous in the family for her wide variety of mouthwatering pies, often carting 5 or 6 pies to holiday parties and family events. She always made a separate pumpkin pie for Billy to enjoy at home.

Billy and Wanda went on to have four more children. A son named Jon Edwin was born on Thursday, March 16, 1952. After Jon, they had three daughters. Rhonda Carol Harmon was born on Tuesday, November 24, 1953. Debra Jo Harmon was born on Saturday, February 26, 1955. The baby of the family was Donna Kay Harmon. She was born March 3, 1959. It was their oldest son, Kenny, who would make the next big mark on the world, as his name was echoed across the country, though not as KENNY, but as SAD PAPAW.

Wanda's secret shortcut for making turkey

Bring 3-4 cans of Crisco to a boil. Drop the whole turkey in (unstuffed) and let it cook 4 minutes per pound. (If you use a deep fryer, follow its timing instead.

Chapter 13

Seeds of Faith
1840-2017

eter and Mary both grew up in families with strong Christian values and morals that would seep into the fabric of time, continuing through to each generation. Peter's brother, John Harman, was a Baptist minister in Chillicothe, Missouri. For Peter and Mary, it began in 1846, when they first stepped through the doorway of the Jellico Creek Baptist Church, with one-year-old KC in tow, as new members.

FRANK HARMAN

Their son, Frank, grew to be a Baptist minister and helped to organize several churches in Missouri and Oklahoma. It all began in Birmingham, Missouri. Frank, alongside John Foster and JP Cooper, bought a piece of land from William & Mary Ewing and soon laid down the foundation to build the First Baptist Church of Birmingham. They worked long and hard to build the church from the ground up. A job well rewarded on January 27, 1888. It was on that day that the church opened its doors for the first time. The bells' clanging sound echoed throughout the countryside, greeting families for up to 5 miles away. In 1901, Frank moved his family to Verden, Oklahoma. There, he raised money to build four churches in the Verden area. The first one was at Spring Creek, 16 miles north of Verden.

RAISH HARMAN

Raish Harman and his wife, Elzie, were members of the Draper Park Christian Church, in the 1940's, where he was an Elder. At home, Raish organized the Metropolitan Church and held services in their living room. As the church grew to 60 members, they changed their meeting place to a 3-car garage owned by the church member, Les Potts. During that time, they raised enough money to buy land and build a church. The new church opened their doors in the early 1960's. Rex Turner was the appointed as the first minister. Several years later, they built a new sanctuary. The church still stands strong today. In 1982, they changed the name to the Community Christian Church.

BESSIE HARMAN

Uhel's daughter, Bessie Harman, with her husband, Amos Harmon, helped to build the Evangelical United Bretheren Church at Wye. Amos was their first minister. It is now known as the Wye United Methodist Church.

As farmers, Bessie and Amos grew a different type of crops—flowers (daffodils to be exact). They planted half a bushel of daffodils in an orchard near their home and sold the flowers at a farmers' market in Little Rock. Two years later, the orchard multiplied into an extraordinary sea yellow. They soon outgrew their limited space. That spring, they plowed them and replanted them in a field that was once a cornfield and was now owned by the church. They paid the church $25 a year for the first five years. They also gave half of their profits to the church. Bessie and Amos contracted with local stores to sell the flowers to them.

They even hired neighbors to help pick them.

In 1976, the Harman's retired their flower business. In their final act of kindness to the community, they donated the land to the town which gave the public access to the hillside. The flowers continue to bloom in March, and the public still loves to visit the "hillside planted in sunshine."

LULU HARMAN RICKER

Being a woman, Lulu Ricker never received the opportunity to minister. Her contributions to the church and her community were reflective of her deep Christian values and deserved to be recognized. She was a literature secretary for 50 years at Davis Circle of the Church. As the owners of a lumber company and a gift shop, Lulu and her husband worked 18-hour days, from 5AM-11PM. Her garden at home was an acre wide. She gave half of her crops to neighbors who were sick or struggling financially. Every Sunday, she visited nursing homes and brought the residents small gifts, candy, fruit, and cake. While there, she read to patients who did not know how to read.

PEARLY HARMAN

Peter's sister, Valentine, had a son named Pearly, who was also a circuit minister. While he attended the William Jewel College in Liberty, Missouri, he served as a Baptist Minister in Gallatin. Upon graduating, in 1911, he moved to Mineola, Texas. This was the start of a long seminary career where he would plant churches in numerous communities with each stop in his travels. His next move was in 1914, from Texas to Bolivar, Missouri. From there, he traveled to Lynchburg, Virginia. That was in 1923. He was the Pastor of the Lynchburg Baptist Church from 1923-1951.

CHARLES LEE HARMAN

Pearly then had a son named Charles Lee Harman. There was a book written about him by Jack E Brown and David Ambristes, titled, "Dr. Charlie: The Life and Works of Dr. Charles Lee Harman: scientist, Christian minister, and educator. Proceeds from the book sales went to the Charles L Harman Scholarship Fund. The fund assisted college students who were pursuing a career in Science or Christian Ministry.

His career choice did not begin with the church. He first had a master's degree in chemistry from Georgia Tech and a degree in Teaching Assistantship from the University of Virginia. It was in 1936 that he answered the call of the ministry and entered the Southern Baptist Theological Seminary. While there, he earned a master's degree in theology. His first position was in Narrows Virginia, where he served as pastor at the First Baptist Church of Narrows. He then became the pastor at the Sterling Avenue Baptist Church in Martinsville, Virginia in 1941. In 1946, he accepted the position of president of Bluefield College in Bluefield, Virginia. He held the position from 1946-1972. While there, he continued to serve God in several ways. He was a:

- Deacon in the First Baptist Church of Bluefield West Virginia.
- Chairman of the Education Commission of the Southern Baptist Convention.
- President of the Southern Association of Baptist Colleges and Schools.
- Moderator of two Baptist Associations in the state.

- President of the Baptist General Association of Virginia.

In 1964 he was awarded the Thomas Gibson Hobbs Memorial Award. The award was named for Thomas Gibson Hobbs, a student at the college's first graduating class in 1904. It was the highest honor given to a student who demonstrated an exemplary record of service in the areas of church community and alma mater.

On May 23, 1966, Bluefield opened the Charles L Harman Chapel. They held services every Sunday and Wednesday morning. Students were required to attend a number of chapel services as part of their college course. The chapel recently underwent updates costing a quarter of a million dollars. These changes included new lighting and sound, flooring, chairs, and carpeting. His years at Bluefield College were known as the Harman era.

Peter's father, Jacob, the patriarch of the Harman family, felt that a deep and resounding faith was key to a good life and sought to instill this in his children. His heart would swell with pride to discover how that one small thought unfolded into an amazing layout of Christian leaders, ministers, and dozens of planted churches throughout the west—a faith that continued to echo behind the walls of Blanchard's Trinity Free Holiness Church.

Did you know? *Until the late 1800's, the Pastor/Reverend of the community church also served as the town's Fire Chief.*

Sad Papaw's Story

* * *

It was on the night of March 16, 2016, that Kenny Harmon became America's favorite grandfather—Sad Papaw. Many bittersweet events arose from his infamous bad burger moment when his granddaughter, Kelsey, posted her popular meme on Twitter. Thousands of people reached out to Kenny Harmon to claim him as their new grandfather. They traveled from nearby states just to have a burger with him. It did not stop there either. People everywhere took the time to think about their grandfather and wondered if they had spent enough time together. Not only did Kenny receive surprise visits from his "new grandchildren," but grandfathers across the country were overwhelmed with their own surprise visits from their grandchildren. People wanted to pull their grandfather a little closer to show them how much they are loved and to have a burger moment together. And through Kenny Harmon's series of books, we would now get to know the true heart of the man behind the image.

Milton Keynes UK
Ingram Content Group UK Ltd.
UKHW050742040324
438876UK00008B/202